The Shape of the Coming Crisis

A sequence of endtime events based on
the writings of Ellen G. White

Donald Ernest Mansell

Pacific Press® Publishing Association
Nampa, Idaho
Oshawa, Ontario, Canada

Edited by Kenneth R. Wade
Designed by Tim Larson
Cover photo by Will Crocker/Image Bank©

Accuracy of all quotations and references is the responsibility of the author.

Mansell, Donald Ernest, 1923-
    The shape of the coming crisis : a sequence of endtime events based
on the writings of Ellen G. White / Donald Ernest Mansell.
        p.   cm.
    Includes bibliographical references.
    ISBN 0-8163-1402-0 (pbk. : alk paper)
    1. Second Advent. 2. End of the world. 3. Seventh-day Adventists—
Doctrines. 4. White, Ellen Gould Harmon, 1827–1915. I. Title.
BX6154.M245 1998
236'.9—dc21   97-18424
                                                                   CIP

99 00 01 02 • 5 4 3 2

This book is dedicated to
Donald Ernest Mansell II, my grandson and namesake

Contents

Abbreviation of Sources

AA	*The Acts of the Apostles*
1BC	*The Seventh-day Adventist Bible Commentary*, vol. 1 (*2BC*, etc., for vols 2-7)
BCL	*Battle Creek Letters*
BEcho	*The Bible Echo*
Broadside1	Broadside, no. 1, no. 2
BTS	*The Bible Training School*
CD	*Counsels on Diet and Foods*
CL	*Country Living*
COL	*Christ's Object Lessons*
CT	*Counsels to Parents, Teachers, and Students*
CTBH	*Christian Temperance and Bible Hygiene*
CW	*Counsels to Writers and Editors*
DA	*The Desire of Ages*
DF	Document File (White Estate)
DS	*The Day-Star* (Millerite periodical)
Ed	*Education*
Ev	*Evangelism*
EGW1888	*The Ellen G. White 1888 Materials*, vol. 1-4, pp. 1 through 1821
EW	*Early Writings*
FE	*Fundamentals of Christian Education*
FLB	*The Faith I Live By*
GC	*The Great Controversy Between Christ and Satan*
GCB	*General Conference Bulletin*
GCDB	*General Conference Daily Bulletin*

HFM	*The Health Food Ministry*
HM	*The Home Missionary*
HP	*In Heavenly Places*
HS	*Historical Sketches*
KC	*The Kress Collection*
LDE	*Last Day Events*
LLM	*Loma Linda Messages*
Lt	Ellen G. White Letter
Mar	*Maranatha*
MM	*Medical Ministry*
1MR	*Manuscript Releases*, vol. 1 (*2MR*, etc., for vols. 2-21)
Ms	*Ellen G. White Manuscript*
OHC	*Our High Calling*
PC	*The Paulson Collection*
PK	*Prophets and Kings*
PM	*The Publishing Ministry*
PP	*Patriarchs and Prophets*
PT	*The Present Truth*
PUR	*Pacific Union Recorder*
Q&A	Question and Answer File (White Estate)
RC	*Reflecting Christ*
RH	*Review and Herald*
1SAT	*Sermons and Talks*, vol. 1
SD	*Sons and Daughters of God*
1SG	*Spiritual Gifts*, vol. 1 (*2SG*, etc., for vols. 2-4)
1SM	*Selected Messages*, book 1 (*2SM*, etc., for books 2 and 3)
SpM	*Spalding-Magan Collection*
1SP	*Spirit of Prophecy*, vol. 1 (*2SP*, etc., for vols. 2-4).
SpT-A	*Special Testimonies, Series A*
SpT-B	*Special Testimonies, Series B*
ST	*The Signs of the Times*
SW	*The Southern Work*
1T	*Testimonies for the Church*, vol. 1 (*2T*, etc., for vols. 2-9)
TDG	*This Day With God*
TM	*Testimonies to Ministers and Gospel Workers*
TMK	*That I May Know Him*

Abbreviation of Sources

True Miss	*The True Missionary*
TSA	*Testimonies to Southern Africa*
UL	*The Upward Look*
W	*The Watchman* (originally *The Southern Agent*, later *The Southern Watchman*)
WLF	*A Word to the "Little Flock"*
YI	*The Youth's Instructor*

Versions and Translations Quoted

Scripture references are taken from the King James Version unless otherwise noted. Other versions cited are noted as follows:

Amplified. From the Amplified Bible. Old Testament copyright 1965, 1987 by Zondervan Corporation. The Amplified New Testament copyright 1958, 1987 by the Lockman Foundation.

J.P.S. From Tanakh—The Holy Scriptures According to the Traditional Hebrew Text. Copyright 1988, The Jewish Publication Society.

Jerusalem. From the Jerusalem Bible, copyright 1966 by Darton, Longman & Todd, Ltd., and Doubleday & Company, Inc.

N.A.S.B. From the New American Standard Bible, copyright The Lockman Foundation 1960, 1968, 1975, 1977.

N.I.V. From the New International Version, copyright 1978 by New York International Bible Society.

N.K.J.V. From the Holy Bible, New King James Version, copyright 1979, 1980, 1982 by Thomas Nelson, Inc.

N.R.S.V. From the New Revised Standard Version of the Bible, copyright 1989 by the Division of Christian Education of the National Council of Churches of Christ in the USA. All rights reserved.

R.S.V. From the Revised Standard Version Bible, copyright 1946, 1952, 1971, 1973 by the Division of Education of the National Council of the Churches of Christ in the USA, and used by permission.

T.E.V. From the Good News Bible, the Bible in Today's English Version, Old Testament, copyright American Bible Society, 1976; New Testament, copyright © American Bible Society, 1966, 1971, 1976.

T.L.B. From The Living Bible, Paraphrased, copyright 1971 by Tyndale House Publishers, Wheaton, Illinois.

Introduction

HUMAN PREDICTIONS AND THE MORE SURE WORD OF DIVINE PROPHECY

We have not followed cunningly devised fables, when we made known unto you the power and coming of our Lord Jesus Christ, but were eyewitnesses of his majesty. For he received from God the Father honour and glory, when there came such a voice to him from the excellent glory, This is my beloved Son, in whom I am well pleased. And this voice which came from heaven we heard, when we were with him in the holy mount. We have also a more sure word of prophecy; whereunto ye do well that ye take heed.—2 Peter 1:16-19.

H. G. Wells's prediction

In 1933 the famous British historian, novelist, and Utopian, Herbert George Wells, better known simply as H. G. Wells, published a novel entitled *The Shape of Things to Come.* In his book Mr. Wells described the history of the world in advance for the next 173 years, or to the year 2106. As a Utopian as well as an evolutionist, Mr. Wells believed that human society was steadily progressing toward perfection. In the struggle for the survival of the fittest, there would be occasional setbacks, but the overall trend would be ever upward toward Utopia. It is not surprising, therefore, that in his *Shape of Things to Come* Mr. Wells described the future history of the world in rather glowing terms.

But in 1939 Mr. Wells had a rude awakening. World War II shattered his Utopian dream. As a result, in 1945, a year before his death, Mr. Wells published his last book titled *Mind at the End of Its Tether* (San Francisco: Millet Books, 1973, iii). The book has been described as "a thin cry of despair." In it Mr. Wells acknowledges the failure of his predictions. One chapter is titled "There Is No 'Pattern of Things to Come' "—a candid admission that his prophecy had missed the mark.

Predictions of psychics

That is the way it is with human predictions. They quite frequently fail. The "Life" section of *The Idaho Statesman* of January 23, 1995, carried an article entitled "Psychics Couldn't See Their Bad Year Coming." In this article, journalist Gene Emery, who has been tracking the predictions of psychics since 1978, found that psychics "usually do horribly," but that "for 1994 they did a little bit worse." Here is a sampling of the forecasts they made: "Frank Sinatra will be appointed ambassador to Italy;" "Madonna was to marry a Middle Eastern sheik and become a 'totally traditional' wife;" "Charles Manson would undergo a sex change operation and would be set free."

Unlike the unreliable predictions of the psychics or even of sober forecasters like Mr. Wells, the Bible offers what 2 Peter 1:19 calls *"a more sure word of prophecy."* The context of this statement is Jesus' transfiguration. Peter was convinced that Christ would come again in power and glory because he witnessed the transfiguration.

The more sure word of prophecy

Peter then says that we have a word that is more sure than his eyewitness testimony. How can this be? Here is the answer. What Peter saw on the mount of transfiguration convinced *him* that Jesus would return to this earth in power and glory. But you and I were not there. We must take Peter's word that what he saw was proof of the Second Coming. Not so with Bible prophecy. We who see the fulfillment of the Bible's signs of Christ's return have evidence more reliable than Peter's eyewitness testimony. We can see the prophecies of the Second Coming fulfilling before our eyes. It is in this sense that Bible prophecy is "more sure" than taking Peter's word as an eyewitness.

The Bible is like a high-seas chart

The Bible is like a high-seas chart by which a pilot guides a ship to its destination. In a similar way, as we study the prophecies of the Bible concerning Christ's second coming and witness the fulfillment of these predictions in our day, our confidence in last-day Bible prophecy, and indeed in the Bible itself, is strengthened. Let me illustrate:

When I was four years old, my parents moved from Rio de Janeiro, Brazil, to Recife, located on the northeast bulge of South America. We made the trip on an ocean liner. On the way, my father made friends with the captain. One day the captain invited my father to come up to the bridge—and I was allowed to go along! All I really remember is the pilot turning a big wheel with many handles. I was too young to notice a large high-seas chart in front of the wheel by which the pilot was guiding the ship. If I had been old enough to understand and had examined the map, I would have seen the coast of Brazil on the left and the Atlantic Ocean on the right as we sailed north toward our destination.

Our ship arrived outside of Recife harbor about two o'clock in the morning and stopped. The city takes its name from a coral reef that runs parallel with the coast, making the channel into the harbor extremely dangerous to navigate.

Mom and Dad woke us children up, dressed us, and led us up on deck to the ship's railing. As I stood by my father, peering into the darkness, Dad pointed to a light bobbing up and down that was slowly coming toward us. He said the light was on a rowboat that was bringing a pilot, who would guide our ship into port. As the little boat approached, I could make out the pilot dressed in white trousers and jacket standing on the bow of the rowboat. Soon the little craft entered a bright circle of light that shone down from our ship.

Suddenly I heard a loud clatter to my right as the sailors on our vessel dumped a coil of rope ladder over the side. As I looked back to watch the pilot, I saw him waiting for just the right wave to come along and lift his little boat high enough so he could catch hold of the ladder and climb up into the ship.

If I had gone up to the bridge this time and had been old enough to compare the harbor map with the high-seas map, I would have discovered that the only difference between the two charts was that the harbor map was much more detailed and highlighted much more clearly the coral reefs and sandbars. I would have noticed that at every significant point the Recife harbor map agreed with the high-seas map.

The Bible is the Christian's high-seas map. Its prophecies show us in broad outline what lies ahead. Christians through the centuries have guided their lives by its teachings, and they know its prophecies are trustworthy.

The Seventh-day Adventist's harbor chart

As Seventh-day Adventist Christians, we believe that as our vessel—our church—nears its heavenly harbor, there are dangerous reefs that could cause shipwreck of faith (see 1 Tim. 1:19), so God has given us a harbor chart to help guide our vessel past the dangerous reefs that lie ahead. This chart is the writings of the Spirit of Prophecy.

The Spirit of Prophecy is a body of writings penned by Ellen G. White, who, we believe, was inspired of God. We believe that just as the Recife harbor map agreed with the high-seas map at every significant point, so the Spirit of Prophecy writings agree with the Bible at every significant point. By comparing these writings with the Bible, we have concluded that they are divinely inspired. The Bible is the time-tested high-seas chart by which we know whether our harbor map, or any other harbor map for that matter, is divinely inspired.

We make no apology for claiming that Ellen White was a prophet of God and that her writings were divinely inspired. But someone may be wondering: Aren't prophets a thing of the past? Weren't prophets only for Bible times? Are God's people in the last days to have the prophetic gift among them? Let us see what the Bible says about this.

The gift of prophecy and God's remnant church

In Revelation 12:17, we read—

> The dragon was furious (enraged) at the woman, and he went away to wage war on the remainder of her descendants, [on those] who obey God's commandments and who have the testimony of Jesus Christ (Amplified).

This is obviously symbolic language, and we believe that the Bible is its own best interpreter. So, let us allow the Bible to interpret the meaning of these various symbols.

What does the dragon represent?

Rev. 12:9, says:

> The great dragon was cast out, that serpent of old, called the Devil and Satan (NKJV).

The dragon represents Satan. So by substitution we can say, "Satan was furious [enraged] at the woman."

But what does this woman represent?

Speaking to the church in 2 Corinthians 11:2, the apostle Paul says:

> I have betrothed you [the church] to one husband, that I may present you as a chaste virgin to Christ (NKJV).

So, Satan is angry with God's church, and he has set out to make war, or persecute, the remainder or remnant of the church's descendants. A remainder or remnant is the last part of something.

Therefore, the remnant of the church's descendants is the people of God's true church in the last days. Revelation 12:17 gives us the marks by which we can identify these people. They (1) "obey God's commandments" and (2) "have the testimony of Jesus Christ."

The commandments of God

The expression "the commandments of God" seems obviously to refer to the Ten Commandments, but let us permit the Bible to make this point.

Deuteronomy 4:13 says that God—

> declared to you His covenant which He commanded you to perform, that is, the Ten Commandments; and He wrote them on two tablets of stone (NKJV).

So God's remnant people will keep the Ten Commandments—by His enabling grace, of course.

But what is the testimony of Jesus Christ?

The testimony of Jesus Christ

The angel of Revelation 19:10, explains to John—

I am your fellow servant, and of your brethren who have the testimony of Jesus. . . . For the testimony of Jesus is the spirit of prophecy (NKJV).

So the testimony of Jesus, which the remnant of God's people possess, is called the "spirit of prophecy."

Concerning this testimony, or spirit of prophecy, the apostle Paul says that

the testimony of Christ was confirmed in you [God's church], so that you come short in no gift, eagerly waiting for the revelation of our Lord Jesus Christ.—1 Cor. 1:6, 7, NKJV.

This passage establishes three points: (1) "The testimony of Christ" is one of the "gifts" (Eph. 4:11 calls it "prophets," 1 Cor. 14:22 calls it "prophesying," Rom. 12:6 calls it "prophecy"; cf Rev. 22:9); (2) Christ placed this gift in a church that is "eagerly waiting" for His "revelation," or second coming; and (3) He bestowed this gift to "confirm," or set His seal of approval upon, not just any church, but upon His true, last-day church.

Prophesying is for believers, not unbelievers

In 1 Corinthians 14:22 Paul sets forth an important principle regarding the prophetic gift. He says that "prophesying is not for unbelievers but for those who believe" (NKJV). In other words, the prophetic gift is for those who, having tested it by the Bible and found it to be in harmony with the Word of God, have accepted its authority. It is not "for unbelievers." It is not for those who do not, or who have not yet, accepted its authority.

This means that we, who believe in the divine inspiration of Ellen White's writings and accept them as authority, are free to use them with those who hold the same point of view. There is nothing sinister or deceitful about holding such a position. Christians of other faiths apply the same principle when they preach Christ to the Jews. Bible

Christians accept the authority of both the Old and New Testaments, but Jews only accept the authority of the Old Testament. As a consequence, Christians use the Old Testament to convince Jews that Jesus was the promised Messiah. However, after a Jew accepts the New Testament as divinely inspired and its Christ as the promised Messiah, Christians are free to use the entire Bible to convince him or her of other New Testament teachings.

Ellen G. White and her writings

Some Christians look askance at Seventh-day Adventists because we believe that the writings of Ellen White are divinely inspired. There are even some Adventists who are embarrassed because statement number 17 of our "Fundamental Beliefs" says—

> One of the gifts of the Holy Spirit is prophecy. This gift is an identifying mark of the remnant church and was manifested in the ministry of Ellen G. White. As the Lord's messenger, her writings are a continuing and authoritative source of truth which provide for the church comfort, guidance, instruction, and correction. They also make clear that the Bible is the standard by which all teaching and experience must be tested (Ministerial Association, General Conference of Seventh-day Adventists, *Seventh-day Adventists Believe . . . : A Biblical Exposition of 27 Fundamental Doctrines* [Hagerstown, Md.: Review and Herald, 1988], 216).

The Bible has words of counsel for such Adventists, and this counsel is equally applicable to those who call us heretics for believing that God has bestowed the gift of prophecy on the Seventh-day Adventist Church in the person of Ellen G. White and her writings. Here is what the Bible says to those who look askance at latter-day manifestations of the prophetic gift:

> Do not despise prophesying, but test everything; hold fast what is good.—1 Thess. 5:20, 21, RSV.

This inspired counsel admonishes Christians not to despise prophesying. But it goes further. It challenges them to test prophesyings. In other words, test the prophets and their writings, and if they prove to be good, hold them fast—accept them as divinely inspired.

But now the question is: How shall we test prophesying?

How to test prophets and their prophesyings

Here is how the Bible tells us to test prophesyings:

Test No. 1: What does the prophet teach about Christ?

Beloved, do not believe every spirit, but test the spirits, whether they are of God; because many false prophets have gone out into the world. By this you know the Spirit of God: Every spirit that confesses that Jesus Christ has come in the flesh is of God, and every spirit that does not confess that Jesus Christ has come in the flesh is not of God.—1 John 4:1-3, NKJV.

The Bible declares that Christ was God—

manifested in the flesh.—1 Tim. 3:16, NKJV.

Thus, a true prophet will teach that Jesus Christ, who was very God, became "the Man Christ Jesus" (1 Tim. 2:5, NKJV)—yet all the while He remained very God. Ellen White's writings maintain this teaching throughout. Anyone who has any question on this point should read her book on the life of Christ, *The Desire Ages.* From beginning to end this book exalts Jesus Christ as God manifested in the flesh, and what is true of this book is true of all her other writings.

Test No. 2: What kind of spiritual fruit does the prophet produce?

Beware of false prophets, who come to you in sheep's clothing, but inwardly they are ravenous wolves. You will know them by their fruits.—Matt. 7:15, 16, NKJV.

A prophet is known by the spiritual fruit he or she bears. In other words, by the kind of life he or she lives.

If a believer in Ellen White's divine inspiration says that she was a good person, that person could justly be considered biased. But if an enemy acknowledges that she was a good woman, his or her testimony carries weight. After all, the strongest argument in favor of a position is the admission of the opposition.

Ellen White's worst enemy (not that she considered him an enemy, but that is the way he treated her after he left the church) was an ex-Seventh-day Adventist minister by the name of Dudley M. Canright.

Ellen White died on July 16, 1915. Before her death Canright accused her of being a false prophet. Yet at a memorial service held in her honor in Battle Creek, Michigan, on July 24, 1915, this man, with tears streaming down his face, confessed that she was "a good Christian woman." Jasper Canright, Dudley Canright's brother, who was also an Adventist minister but who remained faithful to his church, was present, along with other witnesses, when Dudley made the following confession. Jasper left on record the following affidavit (Jasper B. Canright letter to S. E. Wight, dated Februry 24, 1931, quoted in *I Was Canright's Secretary*, by Carrie Johnson [Hagerstown, Md.: Review and Herald, 1971] 105, 106).

Battle Creek, Michigan
February 24, 1931

Elder S. E. Wight
120 Madison Avenue, S.E.,
Grand Rapids, Michigan

Dear Elder Wight:

My brother, the late D. M. Canright, often told me to remain true to the message. He said too: "If you give up the message, it will ruin your life." Many years ago in a public meeting at West Le Roy, where he had been called to oppose the work of a Seventh Day Adventist minister, he made the following statements: "I think I know why you have called me out here. You expect me to prove from the Bible that Sunday is the Sabbath, and that Saturday isn't the Sabbath. Now, I can't prove from the Bible that Sunday is the Sabbath, for it isn't there, and I think I can convince you that Saturday is not the Sabbath [*sic*]."[1]

Then again as he stood at Sister White's casket with one hand in my arm and the other on her coffin with tears streaming down his cheeks, he said: "There's a noble Christian woman gone."

Sincerely yours in the blessed hope,

(Signed) J. B. Canright

This testimony of an eyewitness and blood brother of Dudley Canright is more compelling than the testimony of a mere believer in the divine origin of Ellen White's writings.

Test No. 3: *Do the prophet's writings agree with the Ten Commandments and the rest of the Bible?*

Listen to what Isaiah says:

To the law and to the testimony! If they do not speak according to this word, it is because there is no light in them.—Isa. 8:20, NKJV.

This test consists of two parts: (1) What does the prophet teach with respect to what God wrote—the Ten-Commandment law (Exod. 31:18)? and (2) What does the prophet teach with respect to what the prophets wrote—the testimony of the Bible writers? Applied to Ellen White and her writings, the answer is: She consistently encouraged Christians to keep God's law, and by His grace she endeavored to faithfully keep all God's commandments herself—including the Sabbath commandment. With respect to the Bible, the answer is: Her writings are in full agreement with the testimony of the Bible prophets. Neither she nor her writings ever presumed to correct the Bible. Rather, she and her writings accepted the Bible as it was written and ever maintained the supremacy of Scripture.

Notice what she wrote in this regard:

---

1. Saturday commences at midnight and ends at midnight. The Bible Sabbath begins on Friday at sundown and ends on Saturday at sundown. Hence Canright stated the matter correctly, Saturday is not the Sabbath.

Let everything be brought to the Bible; for it is the only rule of faith and doctrine.—*BEcho* 15 October 1892.

While Ellen White's writings frequently supply enlightening insights, at every juncture where these insights are compared with the Bible, they are in full agreement with Scripture.

Test No. 4: *Do the prophet's predictions come to pass?*

When the word of the prophet comes to pass, the prophet will be known as one whom the Lord has truly sent.—Jer. 28:9, NKJV.

The fulfillment of a prophet's predictions is the fourth test that establishes whether or not he or she is divinely inspired. In due time we shall examine some predictions Ellen White has made, but first let us note that—

All four tests must be applied

The application of a single Bible test does not establish whether or not a person is a prophet of God. Some false prophets may acknowledge that Christ was God manifest in human flesh but fail one or more of the other tests. Some may seemingly live godly lives but fail another test. Still others may profess to keep God's law and claim their writings harmonize with the Bible—and this may actually appear to be the case—for a time—but after a while, either they or their writings fail one or more of the other tests. And, finally, some false prophets may predict things that actually come to pass but fail one or more of the other tests. Hence, to establish that a prophet is divinely inspired, he must pass all four Bible tests.

Predictions about religious conditions in the last days

We have established that Ellen White and her writings pass three of the four Bible tests of a true prophet. The rest of this chapter deals with one of her predictions, which we believe is currently in the process of fulfillment. Many of her predictions have to do with religious intolerance in America and the world in the last days. These prophecies will be the subject of the rest of this book.

Over a century ago, at a time when Protestants openly opposed Roman

Catholics, Ellen White predicted—

> The Protestants of the United States will be foremost in stretching their hands across the gulf to grasp the hand of spiritualism; they will reach over the abyss to clasp hands with the Roman power; and under the influence of this threefold union, this country will follow in the steps of Rome in trampling on the rights of conscience.—*GC* 588.

In the *Review,* June 1, 1886, she explained how this would happen—

> This union will not, however, be effected by a change in Catholicism; for Rome never changes. She claims infallibility. It is Protestantism that will change. The adoption of liberal ideas on its part will bring it where it can clasp the hand of Catholicism.

She explains how the leading denominations in America will bring this about:

> When the leading churches of the United States, uniting upon such points of doctrine as are held by them in common, shall influence the state to enforce their decrees and to sustain their institutions, then Protestant America will have formed an image of the Roman hierarchy, and the infliction of civil penalties upon dissenters will inevitably result.—*GC* 445.

Today we see America moving in the direction of fulfilling these predictions. An article by Gustave Nieburh, captioned, "Religion, Politics Can Mix," states that:

> In evidence of a striking change in American attitudes about religion and politics, a majority of the public now believes that churches should be allowed to express political opinions, a reversal from what a majority believed a generation ago, according to a new nationwide survey of religious identity and political opinion.—*Idaho Statesman,* 25 June 1996, citing the New York Times News Service.

Whether this trend will continue, accompanied by a shift toward agitation for Sunday legislation, which Ellen White's writings predict, as we shall see in coming chapters, we do not know. Nor is it necessary that we know. We base our faith not on surveys but on the sure word of prophecy.

The Bible Belt and the coming crisis

In his booklet, *Flirting With Rome: Evangelical Entanglement With Roman Catholicism,* David W. Cloud says that for more than thirty years (since the 1960s) the Southern Baptist Convention has been reaching out to Roman Catholics (Oak Harbor, Wa.: Way of Life Literature, 1993, 3:4). Until a few years ago the SBC was strongly anti-Catholic and one of the staunchest supporters of separation of church and state in America.

In his recently published book, *A Woman Rides the Beast,* Dave Hunt, who is not a Seventh-day Adventist but sees the danger posed by the so-called Christian Coalition or religious right, states:

> Increasing numbers of today's evangelicals are accepting Catholics as Christians and seem to find no problem in joining with them in the evangelization of the world. That fact is made clear by the very title of the historic joint declaration . . . by Catholic and evangelical leaders.—*Evangelicals and Catholics Together: The Christian Mission in the 3rd Millennium* (Eugene, Ore.: Harvest House Publishers, 1994, 413).

What brings the Sunday-Sabbath issue to the fore?

Besides changes in the religious climate, today we are witnesses to ecological changes that are beginning to affect the earth's climate and portend disasters of enormous consequence. We also see political corruption and moral decay permeating, not only America, but society everywhere on the globe. Notice what Ellen White predicted in this connection long ago—

> As men depart further and further from God, Satan is permitted to have power over the children of disobedience. He hurls destruction among men.—*RH* 16 July 1901.

Notice who is really causing these calamities and what Ellen White forecasts will happen when these disasters strike:

It will be declared that men are offending God by the violation of the Sunday sabbath; that this sin has brought calamities which will not cease until Sunday observance shall be strictly enforced; and that those who present the claims of the fourth commandment, thus destroying reverence for Sunday, are troublers of the people, preventing their restoration to divine favor and temporal prosperity.—*GC* 590.

Seventh-day Adventists, proclaimers of the sure word of prophecy, not time-setters

These Satan-caused calamities predicted over a hundred years ago may come more quickly than any of us expect. But whenever they come, we should be spiritually prepared—and yet avoid being prognosticators or time-setters. Ellen White cautions:

Again and again have I been warned in regard to time-setting. There will never again [since 1844] be a message for the people of God that will be based on time. We are not to know the definite time either for the outpouring of the Holy Spirit or for the coming of Christ.—*RH,* 22 March 1892.

Elsewhere she admonishes:

It is not in the providence of God that any finite man shall, by any device or reckoning that he may make of figures, or of symbols, or of types, know with any definiteness in regard to the very period of the Lord's coming.—Ms 9, 1891, quoted in *10MR* 272.

On the other hand, while avoiding being prognosticators or time-setters, we are to "catch the steady tread of the events ordained by . . . [God] to take place" (*7T* 14) and, when these events do take place, we are to announce their fulfillment to the world.

What this means is that Adventists have *not* been raised up to be prophets; we have been raised up to be proclaimers of the "sure word of prophecy." Thus, as we seek "to penetrate the mysteries of the future" (*3SM* 394), let us "not . . . be wise above what is written" (1 Cor. 4:6, Sharpe's translation) [translation not in version list]. When the Bible and the Spirit of Prophecy clearly predict that certain events will occur in the future, we can rest assured that those events will take place as predicted, but we are to set no dates for them to happen—nor go farther than the sure word of prophecy warrants.

Watch for the steady tread of events

Ellen White wrote in 1907: "I have a clear comprehension of what will be in the future" (Lt 28, 1907), and this clear comprehension of end-time events is reflected in her clear and consistent apocalyptic predictions. The Bible and the Spirit of Prophecy writings give us many cause-and-effect links between events that are to transpire in the future, but how much time elapses between one event and the next is not revealed.

Since "the final movements will be rapid ones" (*9T* 11), all of us will probably be taken by surprise by the rapidity with which some of these events will occur, for we are told that "the end will come more quickly than men expect" (*4SP* 447).

The primary purpose of prophecy

God's primary purpose in foretelling the future is not that we might know the "day and hour" (Matt. 24:36, KJV) of Jesus' coming or when probation will close or when the Sunday law will be passed but that when "the sure word of prophecy" comes to pass, we "may believe" (John 13:19, NKJV)—and rejoice, "for . . . [our] redemption draweth nigh" (Luke 21:28).

leadingtheway.org

jackhayford.org

GEN 19:16   Gal 3:29

We are Abraham's seed!

intercession of prayers - Keep asking for others - God's grace for us.

Joelosteem.com

PRO 3:6   Col 3:15

Rom 9:1

Kern Iref

5151 Stine Rd

27

A CAUSE-EFFECT CHRONOLOGY OF THE COMING CRISIS

The purpose of divine prophecy

I am God, and there is none like me. I make known the end from the beginning.—Isa. 46:9, 10, RSV.

Surely the Sovereign Lord does nothing without revealing his plan to his servants the prophets.—Amos 3:7, NIV.

I have told you now before it happens, so that when it does happen you will believe.—John 14:29, NIV.

Extent of information available

In the prophecies the future is opened before us as plainly as it [Jesus' crucifixion and resurrection] was opened to the disciples by the words of Christ. The events connected with the close of probation and the work of preparation for the time of trouble are clearly presented. But multitudes have no more understanding of these important truths than if they had never been revealed. Satan watches to catch away every impression that would make them wise unto salvation, and the time of trouble will find them unready.[2]—*GC* 594.

The broad framework of coming events

I saw that Jesus would not leave the most holy place until every case was decided either for salvation or destruction, and that the wrath of God could not come until Jesus had finished His work in the most holy place, laid off His priestly attire, and clothed Himself with the garments of vengeance. Then Jesus will step out from between the Father and man, and God will keep silence no longer, but pour out His wrath on those who have rejected His truth. I saw that the anger of the nations, the wrath of God, and the time to judge the dead were *separate and distinct, one following the other,* also that Michael had not stood up, and that the time of trouble, such as never was, had not yet commenced. The nations are now getting angry, but when our High Priest has finished His work in the sanctuary, He will stand up, put on the garments of vengeance, and then the seven last plagues will be poured out.[3]

I saw that the four angels would hold the four winds until Jesus' work was done in the sanctuary, then will come the seven last plagues. These plagues enraged the wicked against the righteous; they thought that we had

2. Although we may not know exactly when the Second Coming will occur (Matt. 24:36; Acts 1:6, 7; 2 Thess. 5:1, 2), we can know when it is near and can understand the relationships of coming events to each other.
Not one of us is immune to the danger of letting the evil one catch away impressions that can prepare us for what is coming. Hence, the information contained in this book should be studied humbly and prayerfully with a mind open to accept that which God has provided for us in the inspired writings. Although a careful attempt has been made in preparing the compilation, this compiler does not claim it is error-free. It is very probable that all of us will be surprised by the way some future events unfold.
3. This broad outline is a framework into which other inspired information can be incorporated. The great, broad events of the future are: (1) the anger of the nations, (2) the wrath of God, and (3) the time to judge the dead.
"The nations are now getting angry." This links the present with the future events outlined. While the anger of the nations undoubtedly refers to troubles among the nations, it more particularly has to do with the persecuting attitude of the nations toward God's people, as will be shown.
"The time to judge the dead" refers to a judgment that takes place *after* the wrath of God. This judgment takes place during the millennium, when "the saints will judge the world" (1 Cor. 6:2; 4:5; and Rev. 20:4).
The statement that "Jesus [does] not leave the most holy place until every case is decided" refers to the close of probation. This is a watershed event and is referred to by various terms: (1) "Jesus . . . [has finished] His work in the most holy place"; (2) "Jesus . . . [steps] out from beteen the Father and man"; (3) "Michael . . . [stands] up"; (4) "Our High Priest . . . [has finished] His work in the sanctu-ary; and (5) [Our High Priest] will stand up [and] put on the garments of vengeance."

brought the judgments of God upon them, and that if they could rid the earth of us, the plagues would then be stayed. A decree went forth to slay the saints, which caused them to cry day and night for deliverance. This was the time of Jacob's trouble. Then all the saints cried out with anguish of spirit, and were delivered by the voice of God.—*EW* 36, 37, emphasis supplied.

Other events that fit in the broad framework

At the commencement of the time of trouble, we were filled with the Holy Ghost as we went forth and proclaimed the Sabbath more fully.—*EW* 33.

"The commencement of that time of trouble," here mentioned, does not refer to the time when the plagues shall begin to be poured out, but to a short period just before they are poured out, while Christ is in the sanctuary.[4] At that time, while the work of salvation is closing, trouble will be coming on the earth, and the nations will be angry, yet held in check so as not to prevent the work of the third angel. At that time the "latter rain," or refreshing from the presence of the Lord, will come, to give power to the loud voice of the third angel, and prepare the saints to stand in the period when the seven last plagues shall be poured out.—*EW* 85, 86.

Events from Sunday agitation to the close of probation amplified

Heretofore those who presented the truths of the third angel's message have often been regarded as mere alarmists. Their predictions that religious intolerance would gain control in the United states, that church and state would unite to persecute those who keep the commandments of God, have been pronounced groundless and absurd. . . . But as the question of enforcing Sunday observance is widely agitated, the event so long doubted and disbelieved is seen to be approaching, and the third [angel's] message will produce an effect which it could not have had before. . . .

---

4. There are two times of trouble. One occurs *before* the close of probation; the other occurs *after* the close of probation. The first period is often called "the little time of trouble." Perhaps a more accurate term would be "the early time of trouble," in view of the fact that the great time of trouble, when the plagues are poured out, comes later. The early time of trouble continues for a "short period." It is followed by "the time of trouble such as never was" (*EW* 36), which will be "very short" (*1T* 204), possibly by comparison.

As[5] the time comes for . . . [the third angel's message] to be given with greatest power, the Lord will work through humble instruments, leading the minds of those who consecrate themselves to His service. . . . Men of faith and prayer will be constrained to go forth with holy zeal, declaring the words which God gives them. The sins of Babylon will be laid open. The fearful results of enforcing the observances of the church by civil authority, the inroads of Spiritualism, the stealthy but rapid progress of the papal power,—all will be unmasked. By these solemn warnings the people will be stirred. Thousands upon thousands will listen who have never heard words like these. In amazement they hear the testimony that Babylon is the church, fallen because of her errors and sins . . . As the people go to their former teachers with the eager inquiry, Are these things so? the ministers present fables, prophesy smooth things, to soothe their fears and quiet their awakened conscience. But since many refuse to be satisfied with the mere authority of men, and demand a plain "Thus saith the Lord," the popular ministry, . . . filled with anger as their authority is questioned, will denounce the message as of Satan, and stir up the sin-loving multitudes to revile and persecute those who proclaim it.

As the controversy extends into new fields, and the minds of the people are called to God's down-trodden law,[6] Satan is astir. The power attending the message will only madden those who oppose it. The clergy will put forth almost superhuman efforts to shut away the light, lest it should shine upon their flocks. By every means at their command they will endeavor to suppress the discussion of these vital questions. The church appeals to the strong arm of civil power,[7] and in this work, papists and Protestants unite.[8] As the movement for Sunday

---

5. The temporal conjunction "as," which appears in several places in *The Great Controversy,* 605-612, connects the sequence of future events in chronological order from the present to the close of probation.

6. This, apparently, is the beginning of the early time of trouble, when God's servants go forth and proclaim "the Sabbath more fully" (*EW* 33).

7. The fact that the church appeals to the strong arm of civil power implies that agitation for Sunday legislation is succeeding.

8. This union of "papists and Protestants" helps us locate this event in relation to other events in a cause-and-effect chronology of last-day events. Thus, for instance, "When . . . [the United States] shall so abjure the principles of its government as to enact a Sunday law, Protestantism will in this act join hands with popery" (*5T* 712).

Testimonies for the Church, 5:451, elaborates on this watershed event: "When Protestantism shall stretch her hand across the gulf to grasp the hand of the Roman power, when she shall reach over the abyss to clasp hands with spiritualism, when, under the influence of this threefold union, . . . [the United States] shall repudiate every principle of its constitution as a Protestant and republican government, and shall make provision for the propagation of papal falsehoods and delusions, then we may know that the time has come for the marvelous working of Satan."

enforcement becomes more bold and decided, the law will be invoked against commandment-keepers. They will be threatened with fines and imprisonment, and some will be offered positions of influence and other rewards and advantages, as inducements to renounce their faith. . . . Those who are arraigned before the courts, make a strong vindication of the truth, and some who hear them are led to take their stand to keep all the commandments of God. Thus light will be brought before thousands who otherwise would know nothing of these truths. . . .

As the defenders of truth refuse to honor the Sunday-sabbath, some of them will be thrust into prison, some will be exiled, some will be treated as slaves. To human wisdom, all this now seems impossible; but as the restraining Spirit of God shall be withdrawn from men, and they shall be under the control of Satan, . . . there will be strange developments. . . .

As the storm approaches, a large class who have professed faith in the third angel's message, but have not been sanctified through obedience to the truth, abandon their position, and join the ranks of the opposition. By uniting with the world and partaking of its spirit, they have come to view matters in nearly the same light; and when the test is brought, they are prepared to choose the easy, popular side. Men of talent and pleasing address, who once rejoiced in the truth, employ their powers to deceive and mislead souls. They become the most bitter enemies of their former brethren. When Sabbath-keepers are brought before the courts to answer for their faith, these apostates are the most efficient agents of Satan to misrepresent and accuse them, and by false reports and insinuations to stir up the rulers against them.

In this time of persecution the faith of the Lord's servants will be tried. They have faithfully given the warning, looking to God and to His word alone. God's Spirit, moving upon their hearts, has constrained them to speak. Stimulated with holy zeal, and with the divine impulse strong upon them, they entered upon the performance of their duties without coldly calculating the consequences of speaking to the people the word which the Lord had given them. They have not consulted their temporal interests, nor sought to preserve their reputation or their lives.

Yet when the storm of opposition and reproach bursts upon them, some, overwhelmed with consternation, will be ready to exclaim, "Had we foreseen the consequences of our words, we would have held our peace."

They are hedged in with difficulties. Satan assails them with fierce temptations. The work which they have undertaken seems far beyond their ability to accomplish. They are threatened with destruction. The enthusiasm which animated them is gone; yet they cannot turn back. Then, feeling their utter helplessness, they flee to the Mighty One for strength. They remember that the words which they have spoken were not theirs, but His who bade them give the warning. . . .

As the opposition rises to a fiercer height, the servants of God are again perplexed; for it seems to them that they have brought [on] the crisis. But conscience and the word of God assure them that their course is right; and although the trials continue, they are strengthened to bear them. The contest grows closer and sharper, but their faith and courage rise with the emergency. . . .

But so long as Jesus remains man's intercessor in the sanctuary above, the restraining influence of the Holy Spirit is felt by rulers and people. . . . While many of our rulers are active agents of Satan, God also has His agents among the leading men of the nation. . . . Thus a few men will hold in check a powerful current of evil. The opposition of the enemies of truth will be restrained that the third angel's message may do its work. When the final warning shall be given,[9] it will arrest the attention of these leading men through whom the Lord is now working, and some of them will accept it, and will stand with the people of God through the time of trouble.

The angel who unites[10] in the proclamation of the third angel's message, is to lighten the whole earth with his glory. A work of world-wide extent and unwonted power is here foretold. . . . The work will be similar to that of the day of Pentecost. As the "former rain" was given, in the outpouring of the Holy Spirit at the opening of the gospel, to cause the upspringing of the precious seed, so the "latter rain" will be given at its close, for the ripening of the harvest. . . .

The great work of the gospel is not to close with less manifestation of the power of God than marked its opening. . . . Servants of God, with their faces lighted up and shining with holy consecration, will hasten from place to place

---

9. Note: The "final warning" has not been given up to this point, but "shall be given." Thus, the "final warning" comes at the *end* of the sequence of events outlined in *The Great Controversy*, 605-612, whereas the "warning" comes at the *beginning* of this sequence.

10. The angel who unites with the third angel and "lighten[s] the whole earth with his glory" is the angel of Revelation 18. He is here associated with the "latter rain," which *Early Writings*, 86, says gives "unwonted [i.e., extraordinary] power" "to the loud voice [or loud cry] of the third angel."

to proclaim the message from heaven. By thousands of voices, all over the earth, the warning will be given.[11] Miracles will be wrought, the sick will be healed, and signs and wonders will follow the believers. Satan also works with lying wonders, even bringing down fire from heaven in the sight of men. Thus the inhabitants of the earth will be brought to take their stand.

The message will be carried not so much by argument as by the deep conviction of the Spirit of God. The arguments have been presented. The seed has been sown, and now it will spring up and bear fruit. The publications distributed by missionary workers have exerted their influence, yet many whose minds were impressed have been prevented from fully comprehending the truth or from yielding obedience. Now the rays of light penetrate everywhere, the truth is seen in its clearness, and the honest children of God sever the bands which have held them. Family connections, church relations, are powerless to stay them now. Truth is more precious than all besides. Notwithstanding the agencies combined against the truth, a large number take their stand upon the Lord's side.—*GC* 605-612.

When the third angel's message closes, mercy no longer pleads for the guilty inhabitants of the earth. The people of God have accomplished their work. They have received "the latter rain," "the refreshing from the presence of the Lord," and they are prepared for the trying hour before them. . . . An angel returning from the earth announces that his work is done; the final test has been brought upon the world, and all who have proved themselves loyal to the divine precepts have received "the seal of the living God." Then Jesus ceases His intercession in the sanctuary above.—*GC* 613.

The close of probation

It is in a crisis that character is revealed. . . . The great final test comes at the close of human probation, when it will be too late for the soul's need to be supplied.—*COL* 412.

---

11. Notice that although trouble will be coming on the earth and the nations will be angry, yet they are "held in check so as not to prevent the work of the third angel," and that it is during this time that the "latter rain is poured out giving power to the loud voice of the third angel" (*EW* 86).

The restraint of the angry nations is described in *Early Writings,* 38, as the holding of the four winds after the angels *had begun to loosen them.* It is this restraint that enables God's people to give "the final warning" (*GC* 611). This clearly suggests that there will be a brief respite from the troubles that have been coming on the earth while the "final warning" is given. (See *GC* 491.)

The righteous and the wicked will still be living upon the earth in their mortal state,—men will be planting and building, eating and drinking, all unconscious that the final, irrevocable decision has been pronounced in the sanctuary above.[12] Before the flood, after Noah entered the ark, God shut him in, and shut the ungodly out; but for seven days the people, knowing not that their doom was fixed, continued their careless, pleasure-loving life, and mocked the warnings of impending judgment. "So," says the Saviour, "shall also the coming of the Son of man be [Matt. 24:39]." Silently, unnoticed as the midnight thief, will come the decisive hour which marks the fixing of every man's destiny, the final withdrawal of mercy's offer to guilty men.—*GC* 491.

I saw that this world was rocked in the cradle of security so that communications might not be cut off from place to place, and that messengers might have full time to carry the message to the children of God, that they receive it and be sealed with the seal of the living God, and be prepared to pass through the time of trouble such as never was. I saw that it must be a time of peace in order for the servants of God to do their work for souls.—*6MR* 170.

Probation is ended a short time before the appearing of the Lord in the clouds of heaven.—*GC* 490.

The great time of trouble and the death decree
The wicked have passed the boundary of their probation; the Spirit of God, persistently resisted, has been at last withdrawn. Unsheltered by divine grace, they have no protection from the wicked one. Satan will then

---

12. During the early time of trouble, the four angels holding the winds begin to loosen them, but Jesus sees that not all of His people are sealed and He commissions another angel to bid the four angels to hold the winds until the remnant are sealed (*EW* 38). During the respite that follows, the angels renew their grip on the winds. Thus, "the nations will be angry [against God's people, yet held in check so as not to prevent the work of the third angel. At that time the latter rain . . . will come to give power to the loud voice [or loud cry] of the third angel, and prepare the saints to stand in the period when the seven last plagues shall be poured out." The wicked attribute this respite to the fact that at last they have passed a universal law against the Sabbath, whereas in reality the respite is the result of Jesus' restraining order to the angels holding the winds of strife.

plunge the inhabitants of the earth into one great, final trouble.[13] As the angels of God cease to hold in check the fierce winds of human passion, all the elements of strife will be let loose.—*GC* 614.

In quick succession one angel after another will pour out vials of wrath upon the inhabitants of the earth.—*ST* 17 January 1900.

When Jesus leaves the most holy [place], His restraining Spirit is withdrawn from rulers and people. They are left to the control of evil angels. Then such laws will be made by the counsel and direction of Satan,[14] that unless time should be very short, no flesh could be saved.—*1T* 204.

These plagues enraged the wicked against the righteous; they thought that we had brought the judgments of God upon them, and that if they could rid the earth of us, the plagues would then be stayed. A decree went forth to slay the saints, which caused them to cry day and night for deliverance. This was the time of Jacob's trouble.—*EW* 36, 37.

Terrible as these inflictions are, God's justice stands fully vindicated. The angel of God declares: "Thou art righteous, O Lord, . . . because thou hast judged thus. For they have shed the blood of saints and prophets, and Thou hast given them blood to drink; for they are worthy [Revelation 16: 2-6]." By condemning the people of God to death, they have as truly incurred the guilt of their blood as if it had been shed by their hands.—*GC* 628.

Though a general decree has fixed the time when commandment-keepers may be put to death, their enemies will in some cases anticipate the decree.—*GC* 631.

When the protection of human laws shall be withdrawn from those who honor the law of God, there will be, in different lands, a simultaneous

---

13. This plunge into the great, final trouble takes place *at the end* of the brief respite following the close of probation mentioned in *The Great Controversy*, 491.
14. The "laws" referred to here are the "general [or "universal" (*PK* 512)] decree" that "fixes the time when commandment-keepers may be put to death" (*GC* 631).

movement for their destruction. As the time appointed in the decree draws near, the people will conspire to root out the hated sect. It will be determined to strike in one night a decisive blow, which shall utterly silence the voice of dissent and reproof.—*GC* 635.

It is at midnight that God manifests His power for the deliverance of His people. The sun appears, shining in its strength. Signs and wonders follow in quick succession. The wicked look with terror and amazement upon the scene, while the righteous behold with solemn joy the tokens of their deliverance.—*GC* 636.

Soon we heard the voice of God like many waters, which gave us the day and hour of Jesus' coming.[15]—*EW* 15.

Probation is ended a short time before the appearing of the Lord in the clouds of heaven.—*RH* 9 November 1905.

After the close of Jesus' mediation . . . . [He] tarried a moment[16] in the outer apartment of the heavenly sanctuary, and the sins which had been confessed while he was in the most holy place were placed upon Satan . . . Then I saw Jesus lay off His priestly attire and clothe Himself with His most kingly robes. . . . Surrounded by the angelic host, He left heaven. The plagues were falling upon the inhabitants of the earth.—*EW* 280, 281.

I saw a flaming cloud come where Jesus stood and he laid off his priestly garment and put on his kingly robe, took his place on the cloud which carried him to the east where it first appeared to the saints on earth, a small

---

15. "The day and hour of His coming Christ has not revealed. . . . The exact time of the second coming of the Son of man is God's mystery"(*DA* 632, 633).

16. Jesus does not immediately leave heaven when probation closes. Instead, He tarries "a moment" in the outer apartment of the sanctuary, while sins that Satan has led God's people to commit, but which previously have been confessed and forsaken, are placed on the head of the scapegoat. It appears that this "moment" of tarrying corresponds to the brief respite before the plagues fall (*GC* 491). It is *after* this that Christ lays off His priestly attire and clothes Himself with most kingly robes. *While* the plagues are falling Jesus leaves heaven, surrounded by the angelic host. The "number of days," during which the cloud bearing Jesus is passing from the Holiest "to the east where it first appeared to the saints on earth" (*DS* 14 March 1846), appears to correspond to the "very short" period of time between the death decree and the Second Coming.

black cloud, which was the sign of the Son of Man. While the cloud was passing from the Holiest to the east which took a number of days,[17] the Synagogue of Satan worshiped at the saints feet.—*DS* 14 March 1846.

A suggested integrated sequence of coming events[18]:

The Spirit of Prophecy seems to suggest the following cause-and-effect sequence of coming events:

1. While the nations are getting angry and during the time they are angry, the elements of strife are held in check by the angels;
   a. Agitation begins for a law enforcing Sunday observance in the United States;
   b. Men of faith and prayer, constrained by God, lay open the sins of spiritual Babylon and expose the inroads of spiritualism and the stealthy and rapid progress of the papacy;
   c. Millions, amazed to hear such words, go to their religious teachers, who try to allay their concerns with lulling words;
   d. Many are not satisfied with these soothing assurances and demand a "Thus saith the Lord;"
   e. The popular ministry, angered because their authority is questioned, stirs up the sin-loving multitudes to persecute God's servants;
   f. The controversy extends to the law of God;
   g. God's people proclaim the Sabbath more fully;
   h. The popular ministry makes strenuous efforts to suppress discussion of the issues raised;
   i. America abjures the principles of its government by enacting a Sunday law as papists and Protestants unite in common cause;
   j. Apostate American Protestantism appeals to the strong arm of civil power;
   k. The Sunday sabbath law is invoked against Sabbath keepers;

---

17. "A number of days" is an indefinite period of time. It affords no encouragement to anyone to try to calculate the day and hour of Jesus' coming. We have been given an abundance of information that can help us correlate the cause-and-effect chronology of coming events. This information can enable us to "catch the steady tread of events ordained by . . . [God] to take place" (*7T* 14) and should encourage us to prepare for the soon coming of our Lord.
18. This sequence of events is merely suggested. Events may not occur in precisely the order suggested, but it represents this compiler's best effort at this time.

l. Persecution breaks out;
m. Worldly Seventh-day Adventists defect to the side of the enemy, and the majority forsake us;
n. Sabbath keepers, threatened with destruction, turn to God for help and are strengthened;
o. So long as Christ is in the heavenly sanctuary, the Holy Spirit restrains persecution so as not to impede the work of proclaiming the third angel's message, and some of the rulers take their stand under the final warning;
p. The descent of the angel of Revelation 18, representing the outpouring of the latter rain, comes to give even greater power to the loud cry of the third angel's message;
q. The great, final test comes near the close of probation as the third angel's message is closing in triumph;
r. There is a brief respite from calamities accompanying the final test during which the third angel's message triumphs gloriously;
s. This respite continues briefly after probation closes, during which Christ is placing the confessed and forgiven sins of God's people on the head of the scapegoat, Satan;

2. After this brief respite, all the elements of strife are let loose, and Satan plunges the inhabitants of the earth into one great, final trouble;

a. The seven last plagues fall in quick succession, one after the other without any respite;
b. The wicked become enraged because of the plagues and issue a universal death decree against God's people, probably during the second plague;
c. This death decree sets the time for execution as midnight on a specified night;
d. In retribution for condemning the people of God to death, the wicked are given blood to drink as the fountains of water are turned to blood;
e. The interval between the death decree and deliverance is called the "Time of Jacob's Trouble," during which time God's people cry to Him for deliverance;
f. After placing confessed sins on the head of the scapegoat, a number of days elapse while Christ is passing from the Most Holy Place to the east, where the saints first see him;

g. The voice of God is heard at midnight delivering His people;

h. The wicked are arrested red-handed in the mad act of trying to murder God's anxiously waiting people;

i. At midnight the sun suddenly appears shining in its strength, and signs and wonders follow in quick succession;

j. The voice of God announces the day and hour of Jesus' coming;

3. A small black cloud that becomes bright and glorious as it nears the earth appears in the east bearing Jesus.

PREPARATION FOR THE COMING CRISIS AND THE TIME OF TROUBLE

Biblical revelations concerning the future

He will dwell on high; his place of defense will be the fortress of rocks; bread will be given him, his water will be sure.—Isa. 33:16, NKJV.

The kings of the earth, the great men, the rich men, the commanders, the mighty men, every slave and every free man, hid themselves in the caves and in the rocks of the mountains, and said to the mountains and rocks, "Fall on us and hide us from the face of Him who sits on the throne and from the wrath of the Lamb! For the great day of His wrath has come, and who is able to stand?"—Rev. 6:15-17, NKJV; cf Isa. 2:19-21.

A symbolic representation of a transition period

I dreamed of being with a large body of people. A portion of this assembly started out prepared to journey. We had heavily loaded wagons. As we journeyed, the road seemed to ascend. On one side of this road was a deep precipice; on the other was a high, smooth, white wall . . .

As we journeyed on, the road grew narrower and steeper. In some places it seemed so very narrow that we concluded that we could no longer travel with the loaded wagons. We then loosed them from the horses, took a portion of the luggage from the wagons and placed it upon the horses, and journeyed on horseback.

As we progressed, the path still continued to grow narrow. We were obliged to press close to the wall, to save ourselves from falling off the narrow road down the steep precipice. As we did this, the luggage on the horses pressed against the wall and caused us to sway toward the precipice. We feared that we should fall and be dashed in pieces on the rocks. We then cut the luggage from the horses, and it fell over the precipice. We continued on horseback, greatly fearing, as we came to the narrower places in the road, that we should lose our balance and fall. At such times a hand seemed to take the bridle and guide us over the perilous way.

As the path grew more narrow, we decided that we could no longer go with safety on horseback, and we left the horses and went on foot, in single file, one following in the footsteps of another. At this point small cords were let down from the top of the pure white wall; these we eagerly grasped, to aid us in keeping our balance upon the path. As we traveled, the cord moved along with us.

The path finally became so narrow that we concluded that we could travel more safely without our shoes, so we slipped them from our feet and went on some distance without them. Soon it was decided that we could travel more safely without our stockings; these were removed, and we journeyed on with bare feet.

We then thought of those who had not accustomed themselves to privations and hardships. Where were such now? They were not in the company. At every change some were left behind, and those only remained who had accustomed themselves to endure hardships. The privations of the way only made these more eager to press on to the end.

Our danger of falling from the pathway increased. We pressed close to the white wall, yet could not place our feet fully upon the path, for it was too narrow. We then suspended nearly our whole weight upon the cords, exclaiming: "We have hold from above! We have hold from above!" The same words were uttered by all the company in the narrow pathway.

As we heard the sounds of mirth and revelry that seemed to come from the abyss below, we shuddered. . . . We heard the war song and the dance song. We heard instrumental music and loud laughter, mingled with cursing and cries of anguish and bitter wailing, and were more anxious than ever to keep upon the narrow, difficult pathway. Much of the time we were compelled to suspend our whole weight upon the cords, which increased in size as we progressed.

I noticed that the beautiful white wall was stained with blood. It caused a feeling of regret to see the wall thus stained. This feeling, however, lasted but for a moment. . . . Those who are following after will know that others have passed the narrow, difficult way before them, and will conclude that if others were able to pursue their onward course, they can do the same. And as the blood shall be pressed from their aching feet, they will not faint with discouragement; but, seeing the blood upon the wall, they will know that others have endured the same pain.

At length we came to a large chasm, at which our path ended. There was nothing now to guide the feet, nothing upon which to rest them. Our whole reliance must be upon the cords, which had increased in size until they were as large as our bodies. Here we were for a time thrown into perplexity and distress. We inquired in fearful whispers: "To what is the cord attached?" My husband was just before me. Large drops of sweat were falling from his brow, the veins in his neck and temples were increased to double their usual size, and suppressed, agonizing groans came from his lips. The sweat was dropping from my face, and I felt such anguish as I had never felt before. A fearful struggle was before us. Should we fail here, all the difficulties of our journey had been experienced for naught.

Before us, on the other side of the chasm, was a beautiful field of green grass. . . . Bright, soft beams of light, resembling fine gold and silver, were resting upon this field. Nothing I had seen upon earth could compare in beauty and glory with this field. But could we succeed in reaching it? was the anxious inquiry. . . . For a moment we hesitated to venture. Then we exclaimed, "Our only hope is to trust wholly to the cord. . . ."

My husband then swung himself over the fearful abyss into the beautiful field beyond. I immediately followed. And, oh, what a sense of relief and gratitude to God we felt!—*2T* 594-597.

In the last great conflict of the controversy with Satan those who are loyal to God will see every earthly support cut off. Because they refuse to break His law in obedience to earthly powers, they will be forbidden to buy or sell. It will finally be decreed that they shall be put to death.—*DA* 121, 122.

World conditions are ominous

The present is a time of overwhelming interest to all living. Rulers and statesmen, men who occupy positions of trust and authority, thinking men and women of all classes, have their attention fixed upon the events taking place about us. They are watching the strained, restless relations that exist among the nations. They observe the intensity that is taking possession of every earthly element, and they recognize that something great and decisive is about to take place—that the world is on the verge of a stupendous crisis.—*RH* 23 November 1905.

Those who hold the reins of government are not able to solve the problem of moral corruption, poverty, pauperism, and increasing crime. They are struggling in vain to place business operations on a more secure basis.—*9T* 13.

The Spirit of God is withdrawing from the earth, and calamity follows calamity by sea and by land. . . . There is assurance in nothing that is human or earthly. Rapidly men are ranging themselves under the banner they have chosen.—*DA* 636.

All are ranging under their respective banners; all are preparing for some great event; all are watching for the morning. One class is watching and waiting for their Lord, while the other class is waiting for what Lucifer may perform of his wonder-working power.—*Lt* 102, 1886 (all except the last sentence quoted in *8MR* 105).

Radical changes in society predicted

As the Protestant churches have been seeking the favor of the world, false charity has blinded their eyes. They do not see but that it is right to believe good of all evil, and as the inevitable result, they will finally believe evil of all good.— *GC* 571, 572.

Fewer and fewer will become the sympathetic cords which bind man in brotherhood to his fellow man. The natural egotism of the human heart will be worked upon by Satan. He will use the uncontrolled wills and violent passions which were never brought under the control of God's will.—*14MR* 146, 147.

What to do and what not to do in the face of persecution

Those who compose our churches have traits of character that will lead them, if they are not very careful, to feel indignant, because . . . their liberty in regard to working on Sunday is taken away. Do not fly into a passion over this matter but take everything in prayer to God. He alone can restrain the power of rulers. Walk not rashly. Let none boast unwisely of their liberty, using it for a cloak of maliciousness, but as the servants of God, "Honor all men. Love the brotherhood. Fear God. Honor the king" [1 Pet. 2:17].—*LDE* 138.

One indiscreet, high-tempered, stubborn-willed man will, in the great [Sunday vs. Sabbath] question introduced before us, do much harm. Yes, he will leave such an impression that all the force of Seventh-day Adventists could not counteract his acts of presumption because Satan, the arch deceiver, the great rebel, is deluding minds to the true issue of the great question, and its eternal bearings.—*EGW1888* 482.

If the payment of a fine will deliver our brethren from the hands of . . . oppressors, let it be paid.—*UL* 40.

When you are endangered because of the spirit of persecution, seek another refuge.—*RH* 3 May 1892.

Slavery in the last days

Slavery will again be revived in the Southern States; for the spirit of slavery still lives. . . . [S]ome who are impulsive will take the opportunity to defy the Sunday laws, and by a presumptuous defiance of their oppressors they will bring to themselves much sorrow.—*2MR* 299, 300.

I am instructed to say to our people throughout the cities of the South, let everything be done under the direction of the Lord. . . . Satan . . . is putting forth efforts to bring about the enactment of a Sunday law which will result in slavery in the Southern field, and will close the door to the observance of the true Sabbath.—*1MR* 397.

Should the colored people in the Southern States . . . work on Sunday, there would be excited a most unreasonable and unjust prejudice. Judges and jurors, lawyers and citizens, would, if they had a chance, bring decisions which would bind about them rites which would cause much suffering, not only to the ones whom they term guilty of breaking the laws of their state, but all the colored people everywhere would be placed in a position of surveillance, and under cruel treatment by the white people, that would be no less than slavery.[19]—*1MR* 397.

Many of all nations, and of all classes, high and low, rich and poor, black and white, will be cast into the most unjust and cruel bondage.—*GC* 626.

Economic conditions and material losses in the last days

God's people should act wisely and leave nothing undone on their part to place the business of the church in a secure state. Then after all is done that they can do, they should trust the Lord to overrule these things for them, that Satan take no advantage of God's remnant people.—*Lt* 321, 1892; cf *1T* 211.

There will be many great failures in earthly banks, and in speculations, including mining and real estate.—*13MR* 236.

Money will soon depreciate in value very suddenly when the reality of eternal scenes opens to the senses of man.[20]—*True Miss* 1 January 1874).

The Lord has shown . . . that it is contrary to the Bible to make any

---

19. The slavery that Ellen White predicts will come in the Southern States will apparently be of a different order from that imposed on the blacks before the Civil War. It appears that the slavery envisioned will be directed primarily against Sabbath keepers.
20. Perhaps this should tell us something about how we should invest our means before this monetary crisis is upon us. (See Matt. 6:19, 20 and James 5:1-3.)

provision for our temporal wants in the time of trouble. I saw that if the saints have food laid up by them, or in the fields, in the time of trouble when sword, famine, and pestilence are in the land, it will be taken from them by violent hands, and strangers would reap their fields. Then will be the time for us to trust wholly in God, and He will sustain us. I saw that our bread and water would be sure at that time, and we should not lack, or suffer hunger.

The Lord has shown me that some of His children would fear when they see the price of food rising, and they would buy food and lay it by for the time of trouble. Then in a time of need, I saw them go to their food and look at it, and it had bred worms, and was full of living creatures, and [was] *not fit for use.—Mar* 181 (Broadside 2, 1849).

Property that was willed to children or other relatives who believe the present truth will be given into other hands. Guardians will rob orphans and widows of their just dues. Those who depart from evil will make themselves a prey through laws enacted to compel the conscience. Men will take to themselves property to which they have no right.—*Mar* 197.

Put away the foolish reading matter and study the Word of God. Commit its precious promises to memory so that when we shall be deprived of our Bibles[21] we may still be in possession of the Word of God.—*10MR* 298.

Problems with labor unions predicted

Unionism . . . is controlled by the cruel power of Satan. Those who refuse to join the unions formed are made to feel this power. The principles governing the forming of these unions seem innocent, but men have to pledge themselves to serve the interest of these unions, or else they may have to pay the penalty of refusal with their lives. . . .

Men are binding up in bundles ready to be burned. They may be church

---

21. Apparently our Bibles will be taken from us, or at least we will not be able to keep them, hence the importance of committing to memory God's Word. Concerning those who fail to heed this counsel, Ellen White says: "Many will have to stand in the legislative courts; some will have to stand before kings and before the learned of the earth, to answer for their faith. Those who have only a superficial understanding of truth will not be able clearly to expound the Scriptures, and give definite reasons for their faith. They will become confused" (*RH* 14 February 1893). On the other hand, those who have hid the Word of God in their hearts (Ps. 119:11) will be "prepared to give an answer to everyone who asks . . . [them] a reason for the hope . . . [they] have" (1 Pet. 3:15, NIV).

members, but while they belong to these unions, they cannot possibly keep the commandments of God; for to belong to these unions means to disregard the entire decalogue.—*4MR* 75.

The trades unions will be one of the agencies that will bring upon this earth a time of trouble such as has not been since the world began.—*CL* 10.

In the world gigantic monopolies will be formed. Men will bind themselves together in unions that will wrap them in the folds of the enemy. A few men will combine to grasp all the means to be obtained in certain lines of business. Trades unions will be formed, and those who refuse to join these unions will be marked men.—*CL* 10.

The trades unions and confederacies of the world are a snare. Keep out of them and away from them, brethren. Have nothing to do with them. Because of these unions and confederacies, it will soon be very difficult for our institutions to carry on their work in the cities.—*GCB* 6 April 1903.

Labor unions are quickly stirred to violence if their demands are not complied with. . . . In every mob wicked angels are at work,[22] rousing men to commit deeds of violence.—*LDE* 23.

Those who claim to be the children of God are in no case to bind up with the labor unions that are formed or that shall be formed.[23] This the Lord forbids.—*CL* 12.

The time is fast coming when the controlling power of the labor unions will be very oppressive. Again and again the Lord has instructed that our

---

22. If there were no other reason for not joining labor unions, the fact that evil angels are working behind the scenes to incite acts of violence should be reason enough why Seventh-day Adventists should stay out of them.

23. The inspired prohibition against joining unions will test the faith of Seventh-day Adventists who work for unionized companies. Some will doubtless be tempted to rationalize that God surely does not expect them to lose their jobs by staying out of labor unions. After all, they may reason, we have to feed our families.

No one can decide for another what he or she should do in the face of this divine injunction against joining labor unions, but more and more as time goes on, our dependence must be on God, who assures us that His grace is sufficient. (See 2 Cor. 12:9.)

people are to take their families away from the cities, into the country, where they can raise their own provisions; for in the future the problem of buying and selling will be a very serious one.[24] We should now begin to heed the instruction given us over and over again: Get out of the cities into rural districts, where the houses are not crowded closely together, and where you will be free from the interference of enemies.—*CL* 9, 10; *Lt* 5, 1904.

Reasons for getting out of the cities now

The time will come erelong when all who wish to avoid the sights and sounds of evil will move into the country; for wickedness and corruption will increase to such a degree that the very atmosphere of the cities will seem to be polluted.[25]—*CL* 29; *Lt* 26, 1907.

Our cities are increasing in wickedness, and it is becoming more and more evident that those who remain in them unnecessarily do so at the peril of their soul's salvation.—*CL* 9.

"Out of the cities; out of the cities!"—this is the message the Lord has been giving me. The earthquakes will come; the floods will come; and we are not to establish ourselves in the wicked cities, where the enemy is served in every way, and where God is so often forgotten. . . . We must make wise plans to warn the cities, and at the same time live where we can shield our children and ourselves from the contaminating and demoralizing influences so prevalent in these places.—*RH* 5 July 1906.

The people who are seeking to keep the commandments of God should look for retired places away from the cities. Some must remain in the cities[26] to give the last note of warning, but this will become more and more dangerous.—*10MR* 261, 262.

---

24. For a time moving out of the large cities and into the country will be sufficient, but eventually even country homes will have to be abandoned. (See *5T* 464, 465.)
25. One would have to be willfully blind not to be aware that this is happening now and that it will become worse as time goes on.
26. Those who must remain in the cities to give the warning are probably people who have no dependents, but even for these the time will come when they must leave the cities and, as time goes on, escape will become more and more difficult and dangerous.

For the present we shall have to occupy meeting-houses in the cities. But erelong there will be such strife and confusion in the cities, that those who wish to leave them will not be able.—*GCB* 6 April 1903.

More and more, as wickedness increases in the great cities, we shall have to work them from outpost centers.—*RH* 27 September 1906.

The cities are to be worked from outposts. Said the messenger of God, "Shall not the cities be warned? Yes; not by God's people living in them, but by their visiting them, to warn them of what is coming upon the earth."—*Ev* 77.

Moves to the country to be made rationally, under divine guidance

For years we have been instructed that our brethren and sisters, and especially families with children, should plan to leave the cities as the way opens before them to do so. Many will have to labor earnestly to help open the way.—*RH* 27 September 1906.

Find a location that has a favorable atmosphere and carry on your work, but keep away from the residences of the rulers of the land. . . . Place not your institutions in the midst of the homes of wealthy men. . . . Nothing is to be done for display.—*10MR* 241.

Those who have felt at last to make a move [to the country], let it not be in a rush, in an excitement, or in a rash manner, or in a way that hereafter they will deeply regret that they did move out. . . .

Do nothing without seeking wisdom of God, who hath promised to give liberally to all who ask, and who upbraideth not. All that anyone can do is to advise and counsel, and then leave those who are convicted in regard to duty to move under divine guidance, and with their whole hearts open to learn and obey God. . . .

Let everyone take time to consider carefully; and not be like the man in the parable who began to build, and was not able to finish. Not a move should be made but that movement and all that it portends are carefully considered—everything weighed. . . .

There may be individuals who will make a rush to do something, and enter into some business they know nothing about. This God does not require. Think candidly, prayerfully, studying the Word with all carefulness and prayerfulness, with mind and heart awake to hear the voice of God. . . .

[L]ook not too strongly and confidently to human counselors, but look most earnestly to God, the one wise in counsel. Submit all your ways and your will to God's ways and to God's will. . . .

Every jot of ability is to be used, and sharp, calm, deep thinking is to be done. The wisdom of any human agent is not sufficient for the planning and devising in this time. Spread every plan before God with fasting, with the humbling of the soul before the Lord Jesus, and commit thy ways unto the Lord. The sure promise is, He will direct thy paths.—*CL* 25-28.

Calamities of unprecedented magnitude

There will soon be a sudden change in God's dealings. The world in its perversity is being visited by casualties,—by floods, storms, fires, earthquakes, famines, wars, and bloodshed.—*FE* 356 (1897).

[B]efore the last great destruction comes upon the world (see *GC* 637), the flattering monuments of man's greatness will be crumbled in the dust. . . . Costly buildings, supposed to be fire-proof, are erected. But as Sodom perished in the flames of God's vengeance, so will these proud structures become ashes. I have seen vessels which cost immense sums of money wrestling with the mighty ocean, seeking to breast the angry billows. But with all their treasures of gold and silver, and with all their human freight, they sank into a watery grave.—*ST* 9 October 1901.

God's judgments are in the land. Whole cities and villages will be blotted out.—*SpT-B13,* 16.

We shall see troubles on all sides. Thousands of ships will be hurled into the depths of the sea. Navies will go down, and human lives will be sacrificed by millions. Fires will break out unexpectedly, and no human effort will be able to quench them. The palaces of earth will be swept away by the fury of the flames. Disasters by rail will become more and more frequent; confusion, collision, and death without a moment's warning will occur on the great lines of travel.—*ST* 21 April 1890.

Great balls of fire fall on dwellings

Last night a scene was presented before me. . . . It seemed that an immense ball of fire came down upon the world, and crushed large houses. From place to place rose the cry, "The Lord has come! The Lord has come!" Many were unprepared to meet Him, but a few were saying, "Praise the Lord!"

"Why are you praising the Lord?" inquired those upon whom was coming sudden destruction.

"Because we now see what we have been looking for."

"If you believed that these things were coming, why did you not tell us?" was the terrible response.

"We did not know about these things. Why did you leave us in ignorance? Again and again you have seen us; why did you not become acquainted with us, and tell us of the judgment to come, and that we must serve God, lest we perish? Now we are lost!"—*RC* 243.

In the visions of the night a very impressive scene passed before me. I saw an immense ball of fire fall among some beautiful mansions, causing their instant destruction. I heard someone say: "We knew that the judgments of God were coming upon the earth, but we did not know that they would come so soon." Others, with agonized voices, said: "You knew! Why then did you not tell us? We did not know." On every side I heard similar words of reproach spoken.—*9T* 28; cf *RH* 24 November 1904.

I seemed to awake from sleep but was not in my home. From the windows I could behold a terrible conflagration. Great balls of fire were falling upon houses, and from these balls fiery arrows were flying in every direction. It was impossible to check the fires that were kindled, and many places were being destroyed. The terror of the people was indescribable.—*Ev* 29.

In the night I was, I thought, in a room but not in my own house. I was in a city, where, I knew not, and I heard expression after expression [explosion after explosion?]. I rose up quickly in bed, and saw from my window large balls of fire. Jetting out were sparks, in the form of arrows, and buildings were being consumed, and in a very few minutes the entire block of buildings was falling and the screeching and mournful groans came distinctly to my ears.—*11MR* 361.

The last opportunity to leave the cities

As the siege of Jerusalem by the Roman armies was the signal for flight to the Judean Christians, so the assumption of power on the part of . . . [the United States] in the decree enforcing the papal sabbath will be a warning to us. It will then be time to leave the large cities,[27] preparatory to leaving the smaller ones for retired homes in secluded places among the mountains.—*5T* 464, 465.

The two armies will stand distinct and separate, and this distinction will be so marked that many who shall be convinced of truth will come on the side of God's commandment-keeping people. When this grand work is to take place in the battle, prior to the last closing conflict, many will be imprisoned, many will flee for their lives from cities and towns,[28] and many will be martyrs[29] for Christ's sake in standing in defense of the truth.—*Mar* 199.

---

27. Leaving the large cities is only a "preparatory [move, prior] to leaving the smaller ones for retired homes in secluded places among the mountains." There will be nothing idyllic about these relocations. They will be traumatic, especially for those who are accustomed to the conveniences and amenities of civilization.

28. The flight from the cities and towns referred to here takes place *after* the assumption of power by the United States enforcing the papal sabbath (*5T* 464, 465), but *before* the close of probation, for it is still possible to "come on the side of God's commandment-keeping people."

29. The time when "many will be martyrs" comes *after* the United States accepts "the religion of the papacy and the law of God . . . [is] made void" but *before* the angel of Revelation 18 calls "the faithful and true . . . [out of spiritual] Babylon," for "the scenes described in the eighteenth of Revelation, when those who are faithful and true are called out from Babylon" comes *after* the vision of "the company that were slain for the Word of God and the testimony of Jesus Christ." (See p. 77 for the full statement.)

Those who apostatize in time of trial will bear false witness and betray[30] their brethren, to secure their own safety. They will tell where their brethren are concealed, putting the wolves on their track.—*RH* 20 December 1898.

Future diet reforms

In a short time it will not be safe to use anything that comes from the animal creation.—*PUR* 7 November 1901.

Among those who are waiting for the coming of the Lord, meat-eating will eventually be done away. . . . We should ever keep this end in view, and endeavor to work steadily toward it.—*CD* 380.

[I]t will not be long until animal food will be discarded by many besides Seventh-day Adventists.[31]—*7T* 124.

When the time comes that it is no longer safe to use milk, cream, butter, and eggs, God will reveal this.—*CD* 359.

[T]he time will come when it will not be best to use milk and eggs. But that time has not yet come. We know that when it does come, the Lord will provide.—*CD* 359.

Great reforms are to be made. . . . But reforms which belong to the future must not be brought into the present.—*HFM* 50.

Angelic protection in the great time of trouble

Some are assailed in their flight from the cities and villages; but the swords raised against them break and fall as powerless as a straw. Others are defended by angels in the form of men of war.—*GC* 631.

---

30. These betrayals by false brethren take place before the close of probation, for angels of God will lead His people to places of safety when probation has closed. The saints will then be hidden by "Christ and holy angels."
31. We see this happening now. Many non-Seventh-day Adventists are becoming vegetarians.

During the night a very impressive scene passed before me. There seemed to be great confusion and the conflict of armies. A messenger from the Lord stood before me, and said, "Call your household. I will lead you; follow me." He led me down a dark passage, through a forest, then through the clefts of mountains, and said, "Here you are safe." There were others who had been led to this retreat.[32]—*Mar* 270.

In the day of fierce trial . . . [Christ] will say, "Come, my people, enter thou into thy chambers, and shut thy doors about thee: hide thyself as it were for a little moment, until the indignation be overpast." [Isaiah 26:20.] What are the chambers in which they are to hide? They are the protection of Christ and holy angels. The people of God are not at this time all in one place. They are in different companies, and in all parts of the earth.—*Mar* 270.

The people of God will not be free from suffering; but while persecuted and distressed, while they endure privation, and suffer for want of food, they will not be left to perish. . . . While the wicked are dying from hunger and pestilence, angels will shield the righteous, and supply their wants.—*GC* 629.

In the time of trouble none [of God's people] will labor with their hands. Their sufferings will be mental, and God will provide food for them.—*21MR* 375.

In the time of trouble, just previous to the coming of Christ, the lives of the righteous will be preserved through the ministration of holy angels.—*ST* 26 February 1880.

---

32. Seventh-day Adventists who have a hideout all prepared for the coming time of trouble, but who fail to make the essential spiritual preparation for that time, deceive themselves. They forget that while they may be able to escape the detection of human beings, they cannot escape being detected by evil spirits. Our only hope of being hidden from evil men and Satan's angels during that time is to be led to places of safety by angels of God.

After Jesus rises up from the mediatorial throne, . . . oppression and death coming to God's people will not then be a testimony in favor of the truth.[33]—*3SM* 399; cf *GC* 634.

33. If God's people are sealed "so they cannot be moved" (*Ms* 173, 1902), if they know that they will not die (*GC* 634), and if angels of God supply their necessities (*GC* 629), why do the saints agonize during the time of Jacob's trouble? The answer is because, although they are sealed, they "know not how securely they are shielded" (5T 475), and there are "hangers-on" among them who fall "all the way along the path one after the other, until . . . the voice of God" (*WLF* 14). These "hangers-on" will appear to apostatize after probation has closed, whereas in reality their apostasy occurred before the close of probation, but their apostasy does not become apparent until after probation has closed. These "apostasies" cause the sealed ones to wonder if they have unconfessed, and hence unforgiven sin, which will reveal that they are lost. Their soul-searching causes them severe mental anguish, but "while they have a deep sense of their unworthiness, they have no concealed wrongs to reveal" (*GC* 620). Even so, "it appears to them as to Jacob in his distress that God himself has become an avenging enemy" (*ST* 27 November 1879). And yet, as with Jacob, they will say "I will not let You go unless You bless me!" (Gen. 32:26, NKJV).

While physical preparation for the time of trouble is important, spiritual preparation is indispensable. After all, what shall it profit a man, if he "escape[s] all these things" (Luke 21:36), only to discover that he has lost eternal life?

Three

C H A P T E R

THE MARK OF THE BEAST AND THE SUNDAY VERSUS SABBATH CONFLICT

The coming conflict in symbolic language

The dragon was enraged with the woman, and he went to make war with the rest of her offspring, who keep the commandments of God and have the testimony of Jesus Christ.—Rev. 12:17, NKJV.

I saw a beast coming out of the sea. He had ten horns and seven heads, with ten crowns on his horns, and on each head a blasphemous name. The beast I saw resembled a leopard, but had feet like those of a bear and a mouth like that of a lion. The dragon gave the beast his power and his throne and great authority….The beast was given a mouth to utter proud words and blasphemies and to exercise his authority for forty-two months. He opened his mouth to blaspheme God.—Rev. 13:1,2,5,6, NIV.

Then I saw another beast coming up out of the earth, and he had two horns like a lamb and spoke like a dragon. And he exercises all the authority of the first beast in his presence, and causes the earth and those who dwell in it to worship the first beast, whose deadly wound was healed.

He performs great signs, so that he even makes fire come down from heaven on the earth in the sight of men. And he deceives those who dwell on the earth by those signs which he was granted to do in the sight of the beast, telling those who dwell on the earth to make an image to the beast who was wounded by the sword and lived. He was granted power to give breath to the image of the beast, that the image of the beast should both speak and cause as many as would not worship the image of the beast to be killed. And he causes all, both small and great, rich and poor, free and slave, to receive a mark on their right hand or on their foreheads, and that no one may buy or sell except one who has the mark or the name of the beast, or the number of his name.—Rev. 13:1,3,11-17, NKJV.

A third angel followed…and said in a loud voice: "If anyone worships the beast and his image and receives his mark on the forehead or on the hand, he, too, will drink of the wine of God's fury."—Rev. 14:9,10, NIV.

Prophetic symbols defined and explained

The dragon is said to be Satan [Rev. 12:9]; he it was that moved upon Herod to put the Saviour to death. But the chief agent of Satan in making war upon Christ and His people during the first centuries of the Christian era, was the Roman Empire, in which paganism was the prevailing religion. Thus while the dragon, primarily, represents Satan, it is, in a secondary sense, a symbol of pagan Rome.—*GC* 438.

In [Revelation,] chapter 13 (verses 1-10) is described another beast, "like unto a leopard," which the dragon gave "his power, and his seat, and great authority." This symbol, as most Protestants [in the past] have believed, represents the papacy, which succeeded to the power and seat and authority once held by the ancient Roman empire.—*GC* 439.

What is the "image to the beast"? and how is it to be formed? The image is made by the two-horned beast, and is an image *to* the beast. It is also called an image *of* the beast. Then to learn what the image is like, and how it is to be formed, we must study the characteristics of the beast itself,—the papacy.—*GC* 443; emphasis author's.

When the Papacy, robbed of its strength, was forced to desist from persecution, John beheld a new power coming up to echo the dragon's voice, and carry forward the same cruel and blasphemous work. This power…was symbolized by a beast with lamblike horns. The beasts preceding it had risen from the sea, but this came up out of the earth, representing the peaceful rise of the nation which is symbolized. The "two horns like a lamb" well represent the character of the United States Government, as expressed in its two fundamental principles, Republicanism and Protestantism.—*ST* 1 November 1899.

But the stern tracings of the prophetic pencil reveal a change in this peaceful scene. The beast with lamb-like horns speaks with the voice of a dragon, and "exerciseth all the power of the first beast before him." The spirit of persecution manifested by paganism and the papacy is again to be revealed. Prophecy declares that this power will say "to them that dwell on the earth, that they should make an image to the beast." The image is made to the first or leopard-like beast [the papacy].—*4SP* 277.

The most solemn warning and the most awful threatening ever addressed to mortals is that contained in the third angel's message. The sin that calls down the wrath of God unmixed with mercy must be of the most heinous character.—*ST* 1 November 1899.

The prophecy of Revelation 13 declares that the power represented by the beast with lamb-like horns shall cause "the earth and them which dwell therein" to worship the papacy—there symbolized by the beast "like unto a leopard."…It has been shown that the United States is the power represented by the beast with lamblike horns, and that this prophecy will be fulfilled when the United States shall enforce Sunday observance, which Rome claims as the special acknowledgment of her supremacy.—*GC* 578, 579.

As the sign of the authority of the Catholic Church, papist writers cite [that, by] "the very act of changing the Sabbath into Sunday, which Protestants allow of;…they acknowledge the church's power to ordain feasts, and to command them [to obey] under sin." [Tuberville, H. "An Abridgment of the Christian Doctrine," page 58.] What then is the change.

of the Sabbath, but the sign, or mark, of the authority of the Roman Church—"the mark of the beast"?[34]—*GC* 448.

The light that we have upon the third angel's message is the true light. The mark of the beast is exactly what it has been proclaimed to be. All in regard to this matter is not yet understood, and will not be understood until the unrolling of the scroll; but a most solemn work is to be accomplished in our world.—*GCDB* 2 March 1899.

No one has yet received the mark of the beast. The testing time has not yet come. . . . None are condemned until they have had the light and have seen the obligation of the fourth commandment. But when the decree shall go forth enforcing the counterfeit sabbath, and the loud cry of the third angel shall warn men against the worship of the beast and his image, the line will be clearly drawn between the false and the true. Then those who still continue in transgression will receive the mark of the beast.—*Ev* 234, 235.

Refraining from work on Sunday is not [tantamount to] receiving the mark of the beast; and where this will advance the interest of the work, it should be done. We should not go out of our way to work on Sunday.—*SW* 70.

Apostasy prepares the way

It was apostasy that led the early church to seek the aid of the civil government, and this prepared the way for the development of the papacy,—the beast. . . . So apostasy in the church will prepare the way for the image to the beast.—*GC* 443, 444.

---

34. J. F. Snyder, of Bloomington, Illinois, wrote Cardinal Gibbons asking if the Catholic Church claims the change of the Sabbath "as a mark of her power." The Cardinal, through his Chancellor, gave the following reply:
"Of course the Catholic Church claims that the change was her act. It could not have been otherwise, as none in those days would have dreamed of doing anything in matters spiritual and ecclesiastical and religions [religious] without her. And the act is a mark of her ecclesiastical power and authority in religious matters.
Signed "H. F. Thomas,
"Chancelor for the Cardinal
"November 11, 1895."
Christian Edwardson, in *Facts of Faith*, (Nashville, Tenn.: Southern Publishing Association, 1943), 292, 293.

Already [in 1889] preparations are advancing, and movements are in progress, which will result in making an image to the beast.[35] Events will be brought about in the earth's history that will fulfill the predictions of prophecy for these last days.—*RH* 23 April 1889.

When the leading churches of the United States, uniting upon such points of doctrine as are held by them in common, shall influence the state to enforce their decrees and to sustain their institutions, then Protestant America will have formed an image of the Roman hierarchy. . . .

The "image to the beast" represents that form of apostate Protestantism which will be developed when the Protestant churches [of the United States] shall seek the aid of the civil power for the enforcement of their dogmas.—*GC* 445.

There will soon be a sudden change in God's dealings. The world in its perversity is being visited by casualties,—by floods, storms, fires, earthquakes, famines, wars, and bloodshed.—*FE* 356.

As men depart further and further from God, Satan is permitted to have power over the children of disobedience. He hurls destruction among men. There is calamity by land and sea. Property and life are destroyed by fire and flood.—*RH* 16 July 1901.

The real cause of calamities and the double role Satan plays

When God's restraining hand is removed, the destroyer begins his work. Then in our cities the greatest calamities will come. Is this because people do not keep Sunday? No; but because men have trampled upon the law of Jehovah.—*3MR* 314.

Satan will continue to act a double part. Appearing to be the dispenser of great blessing and divine truths, he will, by his lying wonders, hold the world under his control; and at the same time he will indulge his malignity

---

35. Note that the groundwork for formation of the image to the beast was laid more than a century ago.

by causing distress and destruction, and will accuse God's people as the cause of the fearful convulsions of nature and the strife and bloodshed among men which are desolating the earth.[36]—*4SP* 444.

Calamities bring on the Sunday vs. Sabbath crisis

In churches and in large gatherings in the open air, ministers will urge upon the people the necessity of keeping the first day of the week. There are calamities on sea and land; and these calamities will increase, on disaster following close upon another; and the little band of conscientious Sabbathkeepers will be pointed out as the ones who are bringing the wrath of God upon the world by their disregard of Sunday.—*RH* 18 March 1884.

Men in responsible positions…, from the sacred desk, will urge upon the people the observance of the first day of the week, pleading tradition and custom in behalf of this man-made institution. They will point to calamities on land and sea—to storms of wind, the floods, the earthquakes, the destruction by fire—as judgments indicating God's displeasure because Sunday is not sacredly observed. These calamities will increase more and more, one disaster will follow close upon the heels of another; and those who make void the law of God will point to the few who are keeping the Sabbath of the fourth commandment as the ones who are bringing wrath upon the world.—*ST* 17 January 1884.

There is calamity by land and sea. Property and life are destroyed by fire and flood. Satan resolves to charge this upon those who refuse to bow to the idol which he has set up. His agents point to Seventh-day Adventists as the cause of the trouble. "These people stand out in defiance of law," they say. "They desecrate Sunday. Were they compelled to obey the law for Sunday observance, there would be a cessation of these terrible judgments."—*RH* 16 July 1901.

It will be declared that men are offending God by the violation of the

---

36. This statement gives an overall view of Satan's strategy in the coming conflict. Manifesting himself as the dispenser of great blessings, he works behind the scenes as a destroyer. In this way he leads those who are deceived by him into believing that in order to be restored to divine favor, Sunday worship must be enforced by law. Such legislation will doubtless seem to be eminently reasonable to those who are unaware of Satan's modus operandi.

Sunday-sabbath; that this sin has brought calamities which will not cease until Sunday observance shall be strictly enforced; and that those who present the claims of the fourth commandment, thus destroying reverence for Sunday, are troublers of the people, preventing their restoration to divine favor and temporal prosperity.—*GC* 590.

Sunday-sabbath laws in America

Satan puts his interpretation upon events, and they [the leading men] think, as he would have them [think], that the calamities which fill the land are a result of Sunday breaking. Thinking to appease the wrath of God, these influential men make laws enforcing Sunday observance. They think that by exalting this false rest day higher and still higher, compelling obedience to the Sunday law, the spurious sabbath, they are doing God service. Those who honor God by observing the true Sabbath are looked upon as disloyal to God, when it is really those who thus regard them who are themselves disloyal because they are trampling under foot the Sabbath.—*10MR* 239.

When the legislature frames laws which exalt the first day of the week, and put it in the place of the seventh day, the device of Satan will be perfected.[37]—*RH* 15 April 1890.

The loud cry of the third angel's message begins

Heretofore those who presented the truths of the third angel's message have often been regarded as mere alarmists. Their predictions that religious intolerance would again gain control in the United States, that church and state would unite to persecute those who keep the commandments of God, have been pronounced groundless and absurd. It has been confidently declared that this land could never become other than what it has been,— the defender of religious freedom. But as the question of enforcing Sunday observance is widely agitated, the event so long doubted and disbelieved is seen to be approaching, and the third [angel's] message will produce an

---

37. Satan's ultimate goal is not merely a Sunday closing law; it is the substitution of Sunday for the Sabbath as the day of worship, first in the United States, subsequently in Christendom, and ultimately throughout the world. Although Satan achieves his goal in stages, "the final movements will be rapid ones" (*9T* 11)—and may come more quickly than anyone anticipates.

effect which it could not have had before. . . .

Men of faith and prayer will be constrained to go forth with holy zeal, declaring the words which God gives them. The sins of Babylon will be laid open. The fearful results of enforcing the observances of the church by civil authority, the inroads of Spiritualism, the stealthy but rapid progress of the papal power,—all will be unmasked. By these solemn warnings the people will be stirred. Thousands upon thousands will listen who have never heard words like these. In amazement they hear the testimony that Babylon is the church, fallen because of her errors and sins, because of her rejection of the truth sent to her from heaven. As the people go to their former teachers with the eager inquiry, Are these things so? The ministers present fables, prophesy smooth things, to soothe their fears, and quiet the awakened conscience. But since many refuse to be satisfied with the mere authority of men, and demand a plain "Thus saith the Lord," the popular ministry, . . . filled with anger as their authority is questioned, will denounce the message as of Satan, and stir up the sin-loving multitudes to revile and persecute those who proclaim it.

As the controversy extends into new fields, and the minds of people are called to God's down-trodden law,[38] Satain is astir.—*GC* 605-607.

---

38. According to *Early Writings*, 33, "at the commencement of the [early, *EW* 85] time of trouble, . . . [God's people] were filled with the Holy Ghost as . . . [they] went forth and proclaimed the Sabbath more fully." This corresponds to the time in the chronology of *The Great Controversy*, 605-612, when "the minds of the people are called to God's downtrodden law." What draws the minds of the people to God's law, particularly the Sabbath, may be the bringing "forth" of the "tables of stone" given to "Moses" (*1BC* 1100), quoted below in this footnote.

"Among the righteous in Jerusalem [in 592 B.C.], to whom had been made plain the divine purpose, were some who determined to place beyond the reach of ruthless hands the sacred ark containing the tables of stone on which had been traced the precepts of the Decalogue. This they did. With mourning and sadness they secreted the ark in a cave, where it was to be hidden from the people of Israel and Judah because of their sins, and was to be no more restored to them. That sacred ark is yet hidden. It has never been disturbed since it was secreted."—*PK* 453.

The "tables of stone" mentioned here are hidden in a cave here on earth. These are not the "original" tables, which are "in the sanctuary in heaven" (*GC* 434).

Regarding the copy that was given to Moses, Ellen White says, "And he [Christ] gave unto Moses, when he had made an end of communing with him upon Mount Sinai, two tables of testimony, tables of stone, written with the finger of God" (Exodus 31:18). "Nothing written on those tables could be blotted out. The precious record of the law was placed in the ark of the testament and is still there, safely hidden from the human family. But in God's appointed time he will bring forth these tables of stone to be a testimony to all the world against the disregard of His commandments and against the idolatrous worship of a counterfeit sabbath."—*8MR* 100.

Regardless of whether the tables of stone given to Moses are brought forth at this time or later, they will be brought forth before the Second Coming, but it seems that this (*GC* 607) is the most logical time for them to be brought forth.

5—S.C.C.

Steps in the formation of the threefold union

The power attending the [third angel's] message will only madden those who oppose it. The clergy will put forth almost superhuman efforts to shut away the light, lest it should shine upon their flocks. By every means at their command they will endeavor to suppress the discussion of these vital questions. The church appeals to the strong arm of civil power, and in this work, papists and Protestants unite. As the movement for Sunday enforcement becomes more bold and decided, the law will be invoked against commandment-keepers.—*GC* 607.

When . . . [the United States] shall so abjure the principles of its government as to enact a Sunday law, Protestantism will in this act[39] join hands with popery;[40] it will be nothing else than giving life to the tyranny which has long been eagerly watching its opportunity to spring again into active despotism.—*5T* 712.

Protestant governments [churches] will reach a strange pass. They will be converted to the world. They will also, in their separation from God, work to make falsehood and apostasy from God the law of the nation [the United States].[41] *RH* 15 June 1897.

---

39. This is the watershed event that marks the formation of the threefold union and the setting up of the image to the beast. This is the "strange pass" that the United States government will reach. *Testimonies to South Africa*, 53 says, "The Protestant government [of the United States] will reach a strange pass."

40. The union of apostate Protestantism with the papacy clearly takes place *after* God's servants unmask "the inroads of spiritualism, [and expose] the stealthy, but rapid progress of the papal power." In the meantime "the controversy extends . . . to God's downtrodden law" (*GC* 606).

The union of apostate Protestantism with the papacy marks a watershed for the United States. From this point on it is all downhill for America; for, as the *Review and Herald*, May 2, 1983, predicts, "When the people of the United States . . . restrict religious liberty, surrender Protestantism, and give countenance to popery, the measure of their guilt will be full, and 'national apostasy' will be registered in the books of heaven. The result of this apostasy will be national ruin."

"National ruin" for the United States does not mean that America vanishes from the world scene; for "the United States" is the "last" "power" "to wage war against the church and the law of God" (*ST* 1 November 1899), and Revelation 19:20 portrays "the false prophet" or beast with the lamb-like horns—America (cf Rev. 13:11-15)—as being "cast alive into a lake of fire" when Christ comes as "KING OF KINGS, AND LORD OF LORDS." Thus the national ruin for the United States begins after America apostatizes nationally, but the ruin is not complete until the Second Advent.

41. See *The Great Controversy*, 605, for evidence that this is speaking of the United States.

Protestants of the United States will be foremost[42] in stretching their hands across the gulf to grasp the hand of Spiritualism; they will reach over the abyss to clasp hands with the Roman power; and under the influence of this threefold union,[43] this country will follow in the steps of Rome in trampling on the rights of conscience.—*GC* 588.

By the decree enforcing the institution of the papacy . . . [Sunday-keeping in place of the Sabbath, the United States] will disconnect herself fully from righteousness. When Protestantism shall stretch her hand across the gulf to grasp the hand of the Roman power, when she shall reach over the abyss to clasp hands with spiritualism, when, under the influence of this threefold union, our country shall repudiate every principle of its Constitution as a Protestant and republican government, and shall make provision for the propagation of papal falsehoods and delusions, then we may know that the time has come for the marvelous working of Satan and that the end is near.—*5T* 451.

An apostate [Protestant] church will unite with the powers of earth and hell to place upon the forehead or in the hand, the mark of the beast, and prevail upon the children of God to worship the beast and his image. They will seek to compel them to renounce their allegiance to God's law, and yield homage to the papacy. Then will come the times which will try men's souls; for the confederacy of apostasy will demand that the loyal subjects of God shall renounce the law of Jehovah, and repudiate the truth of his word. Then will the gold be separated from the dross, and it will be made apparent who are the godly, who are loyal and true, and who are the disloyal, the dross and the tinsel. What clouds of chaff will then be borne away by the fan of God! . . . . Those who have been self-distrustful, who have been so circumstanced that they have not dared to face stigma and reproach, will at last openly declare themselves for

---

42. "Foremost" implies that, although the United States is the first nation to take this step, other nations "follow her example" (*6T* 18). "Though she leads out, yet the same crisis will come upon . . . [Seventh-day Adventists] in all parts of the world" (*6T* 395).

43. In this "threefold union" Catholicism supplies the leadership ("under one head—the papal power—the people will unite to oppose God in the person of His witnesses."—*7T* 182), Spiritualism (through the almost universal belief in the immortality of the soul) supplies the bond that holds this union together, and apostate American Protestantism (through the military might and international influence of the United States) supplies the "persuasive power" carrying out the dictates of the revived papal head.

Christ and his law; while many who have appeared to be flourishing trees, but who have borne no fruit, will go with the multitude to do evil, and will receive the mark of apostasy in the forehead or in the hand.—*RH* 8 November 1892.

When the law of God is being made void [in America]. When His name is dishonored, when it is considered disloyal to the laws of the land to keep the seventh day as the Sabbath, when wolves in sheep's clothing, through blindness of mind and hardness of heart, are seeking to compel the conscience, shall we give up our loyalty to God? No, no. The wrongdoer is filled with a Satanic hatred against those who are loyal to the commandments of God, but the value of God's law as a rule of conduct must be made manifest. The zeal of those who obey the Lord will be increased as the world and the church unite in making void the law. . . . This is what will be sure to occur when the law of God is made void by a national act. When Sunday is exalted and sustained by law, then the principle that actuates the people of God will be made manifest, as the principle of the three Hebrews was made manifest when Nebuchadnezzar commanded them to worship the golden image in the plain of Dura.—*13 MR* 71.

Force is the last resort of every false religion. At first it tries attraction, as the king of Babylon tried the power of music and outward show. If these attractions, invented by men inspired by Satan, failed to make men worship the image, the hungry flames of the furnace were ready to consume them. So it will be now.[44]—*ST* 6 May 1897.

---

44. Notice that the beast with lamblike horns (the United States government) says to them that dwell on the earth that they "*should* make an image to the beast" (Rev. 13:14, emphasis supplied). This is the voice of persuasion—the voice of democracy. "Here is clearly presented a form of government in which the legislative power rests with the people, a most striking evidence that the United States is the nation denoted in the prophecy" (*GC* 443). When persuasion fails, that same beast speaks "as a dragon" (Rev. 13:11) and causes "as many as would not worship the image of the beast should be killed" (Rev. 13:15). This is the voice of tyranny and suggests a radical change in government from a democracy to some form of despotism. Thus, measures which are mild at first, will become "draconian" and will ultimately demand the death penalty for Sabbath keeping.

The formation of the image to the beast mentioned in these statements refers to the image to the beast in America. But the formation of the image does not stop with America. It is an evolving process. Eventually the decree for the observance of the false sabbath goes forth to the whole world. Thus, whether the Spirit of Prophecy is speaking of the image as at first set up by the United States or the worldwide image to the beast, "the same crisis will come upon . . . [Seventh-day Adventists] in all parts of the world" (*6T* 395).

The beast with two horns "causeth [commands[45]] all, both small and great, rich and poor, free and bond, to receive a mark in their right hand, or in their foreheads."—*GC* 445.

The papacy regains its dominion over Christendom

When the Sabbath becomes the special point of controversy throughout Christendom, the persistent refusal of a small minority to yield to the popular demand will make them objects of universal execration. It will be urged that the few who stand in opposition to an institution of the church and a law of the state, ought not to be tolerated; that it is better for them to suffer than for whole nations to be thrown into confusion and lawlessness. . . . Romanism in the Old World, and apostate Protestantism in the New, will pursue a similar course toward those who honor all the divine precepts.—*YI* 12 July 1904; cf *GC* 615, 616.

In the issue of the contest, all Christendom[46] will be divided into two great classes,—those who keep the commandments of God and the faith of Jesus, and those who worship the beast and his image and receive his mark.—*GC* 450.

The world follows America's lead

Foreign nations will follow the example of the United States. Though she leads out, yet the same crisis [over the Sunday vs. Sabbath test] will come upon our people in all parts of the world.—*6T* 395.

As America, the land of religious liberty, shall unite with the papacy

---

45. The United States, apparently, will be the "enforcer" of the law that imposes the mark of the beast on earth dwellers (Rev. 13:14), for "the claims of . . . [Rome's] spurious sabbath are to be enforced upon the world. The Protestant churches . . . will bring these to the front, and force them upon the consciences of men" (*HM* 1 November 1893).
There is no reason for Americans to take pride or pleasure in this prediction, for, tragically this apostasy is "the signal for national ruin" (*GCDB* 13 April 1891). For further discussion on how national ruin results from this apostasy, see above under *Testimonies for the Church*, 5:712.
46. Observe that it is *after* apostate Protestant America clasps "the right hand of fellowship" of popery (*RH* 1 January 1889) that the papacy regains its power and influence over the nations of Christendom over which it formerly held sway. (See *GC* 579.)

in forcing the conscience and compelling men to honor the false sabbath, the people of every country on the globe will be lead to follow her example.—*6T* 18.

Nations will be stirred to their very center. Support will be withdrawn from those who proclaim God's law as the only standard of righteousness, the only sure test of character. And all who will not bow to the decree of the national councils, and obey the national laws to exalt the Sabbath instituted by the man of sin, to the disregard of God's holy day, will feel not only the oppressive power of the Papacy,[47] but the oppression of the Protestant world, who will seek to enforce the worship of the image of the beast.—*RH* 9 March 1911.

The first day of the week, a common working day, possessing no sanctity whatever, will be set up as was the [golden] image at Babylon. All nations and tongues and peoples will be commanded to worship this spurious sabbath. This is Satan's plan to make of no account the day instituted by God, and given to the world as a memorial of creation.

The decree enforcing the worship of this day is to go forth to all the world. . . .

Trial and persecution will come to all who, in obedience to the Word of God, refuse to worship this false sabbath. Force is the last resort of every false religion. . . . We need the same spirit that was manifested by God's servants in the conflict with paganism. . . .

Truth is to be obeyed at any cost, even tho *[sic]* gaping prisons, chaingangs, and banishment stare us in the face. If you are loyal and true, that God who walked with the three Hebrew children in the fiery furnance, who protected Daniel in the lions' den, who manifested himself to John on the lonely island [of Patmos], will go with you wherever you go. His abiding presence will comfort and sustain you.—*ST* 6 May 1897.

---

47. Early on it is the decrees of national councils that enact laws exalting the papal sabbath, but near the close of probation "the nations . . . [will] unite in making void the law of God" (*5T* 523; cf *RH* 23 April 1901).

When the image of the beast will be formed

The image of the beast will be formed before probation closes[48]; for it is to be the great test for the people of God, by which their eternal destiny will be decided. . . .

This is the test[49] that the people of God must have before they are sealed. All who prove their loyalty to God by observing his law, and refusing to accept a spurious Sabbath, will rank under the banner of the Lord God Jehovah, and will receive the seal of the living God. Those who yield the truth of heavenly origin, and accept the Sunday Sabbath, will receive the mark of the beast.—*EGW1888* 700, 701.

The world can only be warned by seeing those who believe the truth sanctified through the truth, acting upon high and holy principles, showing in a high, elevated sense, the line of demarcation between those who keep the commandments of God, and those who trample them under their feet. The sanctification of the Spirit signalizes the difference between those who have the seal of God, and those who keep a spurious rest-day. When the test comes, it will be clearly shown what the mark of the beast is. It is the keeping of Sunday. Those who after having heard the truth, continue to regard this day as holy, bear the signature of the man of sin, who thought to change times and laws.—*BTS* 1 December 1903.

Where, why, and when the mark of the beast is applied

Because a people will not bow the knee to the image [of the beast, by keeping Sunday in place of the seventh-day Sabbath], and receive the mark of the beast in the hand or in the forehead, but will stand to the truth because

---

48. The formation of the image to the beast is an evolving process. It begins in the United States, but it doesn't end there. Eventually, before probation closes, "the decree enforcing the worship of . . . [false sabbath will] go forth to all the world" (*ST* 6 May 1897). Thus, whether Ellen White is speaking of the image of the beast in the United States or the worldwide image of the beast, makes little difference. "The . . . crisis" that Sabbath-keepers will face, at *whatever stage*, is still the "same crisis." (6T 395).

49. The formation of the image of the beast involves a "test" in which the issue is: "Accept[ance of] the Sunday Sabbath" or demonstrating "loyalty to God by observing [the Sabbath of] His law."

it is truth, there will be oppression, and an attempt to compel the conscience.[50]—*RH* 15 April 1890.

When you obey the decree that commands you to cease from labor on Sunday and worship God, while you know there is not a word in the Bible showing Sunday to be other than a common working-day, you consent to receive the mark of the beast, and refuse the seal of God.—*RH* 13 July 1897.

There will be martyrs

By the decree enforcing [Sunday] the institution of the papacy in violation of the law of God, . . . [America] will disconnect herself fully from righteousness. When Protestantism shall stretch her hand across the gulf to grasp the hand of the Roman power, when she shall reach over the abyss to clasp hands with spiritualism, when, under the influence of this threefold union, . . . [the United States] shall repudiate every principle of its Constitution as a Protestant and republican government, and shall make provision for the propagation of papal falsehoods and delusions, then we may know that the time has come for the marvelous working of Satan and that the end is near. . . .

As the approach of the Roman armies was a sign to the disciples of the impending destruction of Jerusalem, so may this apostasy be a sign to us

---

50. Both the seal of God and the mark of the beast are received in the forehead. The reason appears to be because the higher faculties of the mind, such as the conscience, are located in the frontal lobes of the brain. The apostle Paul speaks of those who "have said 'no' to the Truth; they have refused to believe it and love it, and let it save them, so God will allow them to believe lies with all their hearts" (2 Thess. 2:10, 11, TLB). With these people rejection of the Sabbath and obedience to the decree demanding Sabbath work and worship on Sunday has become a matter of conscientious conviction. Having rejected the truth, they have actually come to believe they are doing God service by worshiping on the spurious sabbath. (See John 16:2.) These people receive the mark of the beast in their foreheads.

Others, knowing that Sunday is not God's day of rest and worship, who obey the decree to work on the Sabbath and worship on Sunday, fearing loss of job or persecution, receive the mark of beast on the right hand—the working hand for most people. With these people Sunday worship is not a matter of conscientious conviction, but of cowardice or convenience.

As with the mark of the beast, so with the seal of God. It is received in the forehead because seventh-day Sabbath-keeping has become a matter of conscience with them. These people have resolved that it is more important to obey God rather than man. (See Acts 5:29.) So convinced are they of this, that they are willing, if necessary, to lay down their lives to maintain their loyalty to God.

that the limit of God's forbearance is reached, that the measure of our nation's iniquity is full, and that the angel of mercy is about to take her flight, never to return. The people of God will then be plunged into those scenes of affliction and distress which prophets have described as the time of Jacob's trouble. The cries of the faithful, persecuted ones ascend to heaven. And as the blood of Abel cried from the ground, there are voices also crying to God from martyrs' graves, from the sepulchers of the sea, from mountain caverns, from convent vaults: "How long, O Lord, holy and true, dost Thou not judge and avenge our blood on them that dwell on the earth?"—*5T* 451.

The time will come when men will not only forbid Sunday work, but they will try to force men to labor on the Sabbath, and to subscribe to Sunday observance or forfeit their freedom and their lives.[51]—*MS* 22a, 1895.

The rulers of . . . [the United States] will take their position above the great Creator of the world. . . . Laws enforcing the observance of Sunday as the Sabbath will bring about a national apostasy from the principles of republicanism upon which the government has been founded. The religion of the papacy will be accepted by the rulers, and the law of God will be made void.

When the fifth seal was opened, John the Revelator in vision saw beneath the altar the company that were slain for the Word of God and the testimony of Jesus Christ. After this came the scenes described in the eighteenth of Revelation, when those who are faithful and true are called out from Babylon.—*20MR* 14.

Other events that occur after America apostatizes nationally

When [America] shall, through its legislators, abjure the principles of Protestantism, and give countenance to Romish apostasy in tampering with

---

51. This suggests that at first only work on Sunday is forbidden. Subsequently, the powers that be "will go a little farther and say you must keep Sunday and you shall not observe Saturday" (*1SAT* 127). Eventually they will try to force men to labor on the Sabbath and worship on Sunday, and forbid Sabbath-keeping on pain of loss of liberty and life. (Cf *20MR* 14, quoted above.)

God's law,—it is then that the final work of the man of sin will be revealed. Protestants will throw their whole influence and strength on the side of the Papacy; by a national act enforcing the false Sabbath, they will give life and vigor to the corrupt faith of Rome, reviving her tyranny and oppression of conscience. Then it will be time for God to work in mighty power for the vindication of His truth.

The prophet says: "I saw another angel come down from heaven, having great power; and the earth was lightened with his glory. And he cried mightily with a strong voice, saying, Babylon the great is fallen, is fallen. . . . And I heard another voice from heaven, saying, Come out of her, my people, that ye be not partakers of her sins, and that ye receive not of her plagues. For her sins have reached unto heaven, and God hath remembered her iniquities." [Rev. 18:1, 2, 4.] When do her sins reach unto heaven? When the law of God is finally made void by legislation. Then the extremity of God's people is His opportunity to show who is the governor of heaven and earth. As a satanic power is stirring up the elements from beneath, God will send light and power to His people, that the message of truth may be proclaimed to all the world.—*ST* 12 June 1893.

After the truth has been proclaimed as a witness to all nations, every conceivable power of evil will be set in operation, and minds will be confused by many voices crying, "Lo, here is Christ, Lo, he is there. This is the truth. I have the message from God. He has sent me with great light." Then there will be a removing of the landmarks, and an attempt [will be made] to tear down the pillars of our faith. A more decided effort will be made to exalt the false sabbath, and to cast contempt upon God himself by supplanting the day he has blessed and sanctified. This false sabbath is to be enforced by an oppressive law.[52] Satan and his angels are wide-awake and intensely active, working with energy and perseverance through human instrumentalities to bring about his purpose of obliterating from the minds of men the knowledge of God. But while Satan works with his lying wonders, the time will be fulfilled foretold in the Revelation, and the

---

52. The proclamation of the truth as a witness to all nations *precedes* the enforcement of "the false sabbath by an oppressive law." This is in harmony with *The Great Controversy* 606, 607. It is *after* this that the "mighty angel" of Revelation 18 "proclaims the fall of Babylon" (*GC* 611, 612).

mighty angel that shall lighten the earth with his glory, will proclaim the fall of Babylon.—*RH* 13 December 1892.

The papacy regains dominion over the nations of Christendom

In this homage to papacy [the enforcement of the papal sabbath by law] the United States will not be alone. The influence of Rome in the countries that once acknowledged her dominion, is still far from being destroyed. And prophecy foretells a restoration of power. . . . In both the Old and the New World, the papacy will receive homage in the honor paid to the Sunday institution.—*GC* 579.

The Scriptures teach that popery is to regain its lost supremacy, and that the fires of persecution will be rekindled through the time serving concessions of the so-called Protestant world.—*GCDB* 13 April 1891.

The world is filled with storm and war and variance. Yet under one head—the papal power—the people will unite to oppose God in the person of His witnesses. This union is cemented by the great apostate.—*7T* 182.

Romanism in the Old World [Europe], and apostate Protestantism in the New [the Americas] will pursue a similar course toward those who honor the divine precepts.—*GC* 616.

In the issue of the contest, all Christendom will be divided into two great classes,—those who keep the commandments of God and the faith of Jesus, and those who worship the beast and his image and receive his mark.—*GC* 450.

The so-called Christian world is to be the theater of great and decisive actions.—*7BC* 949.

Satan will excite the indignation of apostate Christendom against the humble remnant who conscientiously refuse to accept false customs and traditions. Blinded by the prince of darkness, popular religionists will see only as he sees, and feel as he feels. They will determine as he determines, and oppress as he has oppressed. Liberty of conscience, which has cost so great a sacrifice, will no longer be respected. The church and the world will unite, and the world will lend to the church power to crush out the right of the people to worship God according to His Word.—*ST* 8 November 1899.

The Bible declares that before the coming of the Lord, Satan will work "with all power and signs and lying wonders, and with all deceivableness of unrighteousness;" and they that "receive not the love of the truth, that they might be saved, will be left to receive "strong delusion, that they should believe a lie." 2 Thessalonians 2:9-11. Not until this condition shall be reached, and the union of the church with the world shall by fully accomplished throughout Christendom, will the fall of Babylon be complete. The change is a progressive one, and the perfect fulfillment of Revelation 14:9 is yet future.—*GC* 389.

The law for the observance of the first day of the week is the production of an apostate Christendom. Sunday is a child of the papacy, exalted by the Christian world above the sacred day of God's rest. In no case are God's people to pay it homage.—*9T* 235.

Nations will be stirred to their very center. Support will be withdrawn from those who proclaim God's only standard of righteousness, the only sure test of character. And all who will not bow to the decree of the national councils[53] and obey the national laws to exalt the sabbath instituted by the man of sin, to the disregard of God's holy day, will feel, not the oppressive power of popery alone, but of the Protestant world, the image of the beast.—*2SM* 380.

The whole world becomes involved

The claims of . . . [Rome's] spurious sabbath are to be enforced upon the world.[54] The Protestant churches, having received doctrines which the word of God condemns, will bring these to the front, and force them upon

---

53. Influenced by America's example, the "national councils" of other nations enact laws substituting Sunday for the Sabbath.
54. This is not Protestantism's mere enforcement of Sunday worship on Americans but "upon the world." The "enforce[r]" of "this spurious sabbath" is apostate Protestantism, working through the United States.

the consciences of men, just as the papal authorities urged their dogmas upon the advocates of truth in Luther's time.—*HM* 1 November 1893.

"These have one mind." There will be a universal bond of union, one great harmony, a confederacy of Satan's forces.[55] "And shall give their power and strength unto the beast." Thus is manifested the same arbitrary, oppressive power against religious liberty, freedom to worship God according to the dictates of conscience, as was manifested by the papacy, when in the past it persecuted those who dared to refuse to conform with the religious rites and ceremonies of Romanism.

In the warfare to be waged in the last days there will be united, in opposition to God's people, all the corrupt powers that have apostatized from allegiance to the law of Jehovah. In this warfare the Sabbath of the fourth commandment will be the great point at issue; for in the Sabbath commandment the great Lawgiver identifies Himself as the Creator of the heavens and the earth.—*7BC* 983.

The image of the beast is set up for all to worship

The deceptions of Satan will flood the world. The man of sin [the papal hierarchy] has instituted a spurious sabbath, and the Protestant world has taken this child of the papacy and cradled and nurtured it. Satan means to make all nations drink of the wine of the wrath of the fornication of Babylon. . . . The first day of the week is to be exalted and presented to all for observance.—*RH* 4 April 1890.

The first day of the week, a common working day, possessing no sanctity whatever, will be set up as was the [golden] image of Babylon. All nations and tongues and peoples will be commanded to worship this spurious sabbath. . . . The decree enforcing the worship of this day is to go forth to all the world. . . .

Trial and persecution will come to all who, in obedience to the Word of

---

55. Spiritualism will very likely play a crucial role in the exaltation of Sunday throughout Christendom and the rest of the world through the near-universal belief in the immortality of the soul. It seems likely that in the calamities to come, many will lose their lives, and evil spirits impersonating the deceased will convince believers in soul-survival that these disasters are caused by "the desecration of Sunday" (*GC* 592).

God, refuse to worship this false sabbath. Force is the last resort of every false religion. At first it tries attraction, as . . . [Nebuchadnezzar] king of Babylon tried the power of music and outward show. If these attractions, invented by men inspired by Satan, failed to make men worship the image, the hungry flames of the furnace were ready to consume them. So it will be now. The Papacy has exercised her power to compel men to obey her, and she will continue to do so. We need the same spirit that was manifested by God's servants in the conflict with paganism.—*ST* 6 May 1897.

The universal Sunday-sabbath law

The substitution of the laws of men for the law of God, the exaltation, by merely human authority, of Sunday in place of the Bible Sabbath, is the last act in the drama. When this substitution becomes universal, God will reveal Himself.—*7T* 141.

The substitution of the false for the true is the last act in the drama. When this substitution becomes universal,[56] God will reveal himself.[57] When the laws of men are exalted aobve the laws of God, when the powers of this earth try to force men to keep the first day of the week, know that the time has come for God to work. He will arise in His majesty, and will shake terribly the earth.—*RH* 23 April 1901.

God keeps a reckoning with the nations. Through every century of this world's history evil workers have been treasuring up wrath against the day of wrath; and when the time fully comes that iniquity shall have reached the

---

56. It is evident from the foregoing statements that what begins as agitation for a Sunday law in the United States (*GC* 605) climaxes in a universal law decreeing Sunday sacredness. All nations join in substituting Sunday in place of the Bible Sabbath. This occurs shortly *before* the close of probation. The death decree, which is also "universal" (*PK* 512) and is issued after the close of probation (*EW* 36, 37; cf *GC* 631), is apparently based on the universal law substituting the false sabbath for God's day of rest.

57. The following statement clarifies when it is that God rises up to punish the wicked for making void His law: "When the wicked shall have filled up their cup of iniquity [in other words, when probation closes] then the Lord will rise out of his place to punish the inhabitants of the earth. . . . The supreme Governor of the universe will reveal to men who have made void His law that His authority will be maintained" (*3MR* 216). The Lord doesn't immediately pour out the plagues after the nations unite in making void His law; He waits for a brief period, even after the close of probation.

stated boundary of God'' mercy, His forbearance will cease. When the accumulated figures in heaven'' record book shall mark the sum of transgression complete, wrath will come, unmixed with mercy, and then it will be seen what a tremendous thing it is to have worn out the divine patience. This crisis will be reached when the nations shall unite in making void God's law.—*5T* 524.

It is in a crisis that character is revealed. . . . The great final test comes at the close of human probation.—*COL* 412.

The righteous and the wicked will still be living upon the earth in their mortal state.—men will be planting and building, eating and drinking, all unconscious that the final, irrevocable decision has been pronounced in the sanctuary above. Before the flood, after Noah entered the ark, God shut him in, and shut the ungodly out; but for seven days the people, knowing not that their doom was fixed, continued their careless, pleasure-loving life, and mocked the warnings of impending judgment. "So," says the Saviour, "shall also the coming of the Son of man be."[58] Silently, unnoticed as the midnight thief, will come the decisive hour which marks the fixing of every man's destiny, the final withdrawal of mercy's offer to guilty men.—*GC* 491.

A worldwide death decree

I saw the saints leaving the cities and villages, and associating together in companies, and living in the most solitary places. Angels provided them food and water, while the wicked were suffering from hunger and thirst. Then I saw the leading men of the earth consulting together, and Satan and his angels busy around them. I saw a writing, copies of which were scattered in different parts of the land, giving orders that unless the saints should yield their peculiar faith, give up the Sabbath, and observe the first

---

58. Apparently there will be a brief universal respite *following* the universal substitution of Sunday for the Sabbath; for, *when* probation closes "men will be planting and building, eating and drinking." It is during this respite, but *before* probation closes, that the third angel's message, with the added power of the latter rain, triumphs.
The wicked attribute this respite to the fact that they have finally and universally substituted Sunday for the Sabbath, but in reality it is the angels restraining the winds of strife. God's people see this as their opportunity to give the "final warning" (*GC* 611, 612).

day of the week, the people were at liberty after a certain time to put them to death.—*EW* 282, 283.

Especially will the wrath of man be aroused against those who hallow the Sabbath of the fourth commandment; and at last a universal decree will denounce these as deserving of death.—*PK* 512.

The plagues fall on those with the mark of the beast

When Christ ceases His intercession in the sanctuary, the unmingled wrath threatened against those who worship the beast and his image and receive his mark, will be poured out. . . . Says the revelator, in describing these terrific scourges, "There fell a noisome and grievous sore upon the men which had the mark of the beast, and upon them which worshiped his image."—*GC* 627, 628.

God's people are delivered

When the protection of human laws shall be withdrawn from those who honor the law of God, there will be, in different lands, a simultaneous movement for their destruction. As the time appointed in the decree draws near, the people will conspire to root out the hated sect. It will be determined to strike in one night a decisive blow, which shall utterly silence the voice of dissent and reproof.—*GC* 635.

It was at midnight that God chose to deliver His people. As the wicked were mocking around them, suddenly the sun appeared, shining in his strength, and the moon stood still. The wicked looked upon the scene with amazement, while the saints beheld with solemn joy the tokens of their deliverance. Signs and wonders followed in quick succession. Everything seemed turned out of its natural course. The streams ceased to flow. Dark, heavy clouds came up and clashed against each other. But there was one clear place of settled glory, whence came the voice of God like many waters, shaking the heavens and the earth. There was a mighty earthquake. The graves were opened, and those who had died in faith under the third angel's message, keeping the Sabbath, came forth from their dusty beds, glorified, to hear the covenant of peace that God was to make with those who had kept His law.—*EW* 285.

The original tables of stone appear in the sky

Through a rift in the clouds, there beams a star whose brilliancy is increased fourfold in contrast with the darkness. It speaks hope and joy to the faithful, but severity and wrath to the transgressors of God's law. Those who have sacrificed all for Christ are now secure. . . . Their voices rise in triumphant song: "God is our refuge and strength, a very present help in trouble. . . ." [Ps. 46:1]

While these words of holy trust ascend to God, the clouds sweep back, and the starry heavens are seen. . . . Then there appears against the sky a hand holding two tablets of stone folded together. . . . That holy law . . . is now revealed to men as the rule of judgment. . . . Memory is aroused, the darkness of superstition and heresy is swept from every mind. . . .

It is impossible to describe the horror and despair of those who have trampled upon God's holy requirements. . . . They have endeavored to compel God's people to profane His Sabbath. Now they are condemned by that law which they have despised.—*GC* 638-640.

When God's temple in heaven is opened, what a triumphant time that will be for all who have been faithful and true! In the temple will be seen the ark of the testament in which were placed the two tables of stone on which are written God's law. These tables of stone will be brought forth from their hiding place, and on them will be seen the Ten Commandments engraved by the finger of God. These tables of stone now lying in the ark of the testament will be a convincing testimony to the truth and binding claims of God's law.—*7BC* 972.

[A]s God spoke the day and the hour of Jesus' coming and delivered the everlasting covenant to His people, He spoke one sentence, and then paused, while the words were rolling through the earth. The Israel of God stood with their eyes fixed upward, listening to the words as they came from the mouth of Jehovah, and rolled through the earth like pearls of loudest thunder. It was awfully solemn. And at the end of every sentence the saints shouted, "Glory! Alleluia!" Their countenances were lighted up with the glory of God. . . . The wicked could not look on them for the glory. And when the never-ending blessing was pronounced on those who had honored God in keeping His Sabbath holy, there was a mighty shout of victory over the beast and over his image.—*EW* 34.

[God's people] have walked in the fiery furnace in the world, heated intensely by the passions and caprices of men who would enforce upon them the worship of the beast and his image, who would compel them to be disloyal to the God of heaven. They have come from the mountains, from the rocks, from the dens and caves of the earth, from dungeons, from prisons, from secret councils, from the torture chamber, from hovels, from garrets. They have passed through sore affliction, deep self-denial, and deep disappointment. They are no longer to be the sport and ridicule of wicked men. They are to be no longer mean and sorrowful in the eyes of those who despise them.—*2MR* 210.

Upon the crystal sea before the throne, that sea of glass as it were mingled with fire,—so resplendent is it with the glory of God,—are gathered the company that have "gotten the victory over the beast, and over his image, and over his mark, and over the number of his name." With the Lamb upon Mount Zion, "having the harps of God," they stand, the hundred and forty and four thousand that were redeemed from among men; and there is heard, as the sound of many waters, and as the sound of a great thunder, "the voice of harpers harping with their harps." And they sing "a new song" before the throne, a song which no man can learn save the hundred and forty and four thousand. It is the song of Moses and the Lamb—a song of deliverance. None but the hundred and forty-four thousand can learn that song; for it is the song of their experience—an experience such as no other company have ever had.—*GC* 648, 649.

THE TRIALS AND TRIUMPH OF THE THIRD ANGEL'S MESSAGE

Patient endurance in the face of persecution

Remember the words that I spoke to you: "No servant is greater than his master." If they persecuted me, they will persecute you also.—John 15:20, NIV.

The time will come that whoever kills you will think he offers God service.—John 16:2, NKJV.

They will deliver you up to councils, and you will be beaten in the synagogues. And you will be brought before rulers and kings for My sake, for a testimony to them. . . . But when they arrest you and deliver you up, do not worry beforehand, or premeditate what you will speak. But whatsoever is given you in that hour, speak that; for it is not you who speak, but the Holy Spirit. Now brother will betray brother to death, and a father his child; and children will rise up against parents and cause them to be put to death. And you will be hated by all men for My name's sake. But he who endures to the end shall be saved.—Mark 13:9, 11-13, NKJV.

When He opened the fifth seal, I saw under the altar the souls of those who had been slain for the word of God and for the testimony which they held.—Rev. 6:9, NKJV.

I saw the souls of those who had been beheaded for the testimony of Jesus, and for the Word of God, those who did not worship the beast nor his image, and who did not receive his brand upon their brow, or hand. And they lived and reigned with Christ for a thousand years.—Rev. 20:4, Montgomery.

This God is our God for ever and ever: he will be our guide even unto death.—Ps. 48:14.

Be faithful, even to the point of death, and I will give you the crown of life.—Rev. 2:10, NIV.

Opposition and persecution of Adventists predicted

Severe trials will soon come upon the people of God in this and other countries.—*RH* 13 March 1886.

How few, even among those who claim to believe in present truth, understand the signs of the times, or what they are to experience before the end.—*RH* 4 April 1893.

Now we seem to be unnoticed, but this will not always be. Movements are at work to bring us to the front, and if our theories of truth can be picked to pieces by . . . the world's greatest men, it will be done.—*Ev* 69; *Lt* 6, 1886).

We do not know how soon we shall be singled out as not being law-abiding citizens, because the prince of the power of the air is getting possession of the minds of men. We can choose between obeying the powers that be, and dishonoring God, or disobeying the powers that be, and honoring God. . . . It makes every difference whether we are on God's side of the question or not. You may be summoned to the courts, and in these emergencies think on the Saviour's promise: "I am there." . . . And we can stand there though the whole world may be arrayed against us.—*UL* 101; *Ms* 11, 1893).

The law of God, through the agency of Satan, is to be made void. In our land of boasted freedom [America], religious liberty will come to an end. The contest will be decided over the Sabbath question, which will agitate the whole world.—*HM* 2 February 1890.

In a Sunday Law there is possibility for great suffering to those who observe the seventh day. The working out of Satan's plans will bring persecution to the people of God. But the faithful servants of God need not fear the outcome of the conflict. If they will follow the pattern set for them in the life of Christ, if they will be true to the requirements of God, their reward will be eternal life, a life that measures with the life of God.—*RH* 30 September 1909.

Whenever persecution takes place, the spectators make decisions either for or against Christ.—*RH* 20 December 1898.

Eavesdropping on a satanic strategy session

As the people of God approach the perils of the last days, Satan holds earnest consultation with his angels as to the most successful plan of overthrowing their faith. . . .

Says the great deceiver: . . .

"The Sabbath is the great question which is to decide the destiny of souls. We must exalt the sabbath of our creating. We have caused it to be accepted by both worldlings and church members; now the church must be led to unite with the world in its support. We must work by signs and wonders to blind their eyes to the truth, and lead them to lay aside reason and the fear of God and follow custom and tradition.

"I will influence popular ministers to turn the attention of their hearers from the commandments of God. . . .

"But our principal concern is to silence this sect of Sabbath keepers. We must excite popular indignation against them. We will enlist great men and worldly-wise men upon our side, and induce those in authority to carry out our purposes. Then the Sabbath which I have set up shall be enforced by laws the most severe and exacting. Those who disregard them shall be driven out from the cities and villages, and made to suffer hunger and privation. When once we have the power, we will show what we can do with those who will not swerve from their allegiance to God. . . . [N]ow that we are bringing the Protestant churches and the world into harmony with this right arm of our strength, we will finally have a law to exterminate all who will not submit to our authority. When death shall be made the penalty[59] of violating our sabbath, then many who are now ranked with commandment keepers will come over to our side."—*4SP* 337, 338.

The ordeal before us

It is often the case that trouble is greater in anticipation than in reality; but this is not true of the crisis before us. The most vivid presentation cannot reach the magnitude of the ordeal.—*GC* 622.

Many will be laid away to sleep in Jesus before the fiery ordeal of the time of trouble shall come upon our world.—*GCDB* 26 February 1897.

Many little ones are to be laid away before the time of trouble. We shall see our children again. We shall meet them and know them in the heavenly courts.—*2SM* 259.

We are to be brought into strait and trying places, and the many children brought into the world will in mercy be taken away before the time of trouble comes.—*3SM* 419.

How to deal with Sunday laws when they come

[We are] not to provoke those who have accepted the spurious sabbath, an institution of the Papacy, in the place of God's holy Sabbath. Their not having the Bible arguments in their favor makes them all the more angry

---

59. The death penalty mentioned here is not the "universal [death] decree" (*PK* 512; *GC* 631), for the worldwide death decree is issued *after* the close of probation (*EW* 36, 37). The martyrdoms resulting from the imposition of the death penalty occur *before* the close of probation; for, "After Jesus rises up from the mediatorial throne, every case will be decided, and oppression and death coming to God's people will not then be a testimony in favor of the truth" (*3SM* 399).

and determined to supply the place of arguments that are wanting in the Word of God by the power of their might. The force of persecution follows the steps of the dragon. Therefore great care should be exercised to give no provocation. And again, let us as a people, as far as possible, cleanse the camp of moral defilement and aggravating sins.—*3SM 384*.

It is not wise to find fault continually with what is done by the rulers of government. It is not our work to attack individuals or institutions. . . .

The time will come when unguarded expressions of a denunciatory character, that have been carelessly spoken or written by our brethren, will be used by our enemies to condemn us. These will not be used merely to condemn those who made the statements, but will be charged upon the whole body of Adventists. Our accusers will say that on such and such a day one of our responsible men said thus and so against the administration of the laws of this government.—*6T 394, 395*.

The time will come when we shall be called to stand before kings and rulers, magistrates and powers, in vindication of the truth. Then it will be a surprise to those witnesses to learn that their positions, their words, the very expressions made in a careless manner or thoughtless way, when attacking error or advancing truth—expressions that they had not thought would be remembered—will be reproduced, and they will be confronted with them, and their enemies will have the advantage, putting their own construction on these words that were spoken unadvisedly.—*3SM 403, 404*.

We should not go out of our way to make hard thrusts at the Catholics. Among the Catholics are many who are most conscientious Christians.—*Lt 11, 1895, quoted in 16MR 161*.

All sharp thrusts will come back upon us in double measure when the power is in the hands of those who can exercise it for our injury.—*RH 16 March 1911*.

The loud cry followed by persecution

As the time comes for . . . [the third angel's message] to be given with greatest power, . . . Men of faith and prayer will be constrained to go forth with holy zeal, declaring the words which God gives them. The sins of Babylon will be laid open. The fearful results of enforcing the observances of the church by civil authority, the inroads of Spiritualism, the stealthy but rapid rise of the papal power,—all will be unmasked. By these solemn warnings the people will be stirred. Thousands upon thousands will listen who have never heard words like these. . . . As the people go to their former teachers with the eager inquiry, Are these things so? the ministers present fables, prophesy smooth things. . . . But since many refuse to be satisfied with the mere authority of men, and demand a plain "Thus saith the Lord," the popular ministry . . . filled with anger as their authority is questioned, will denounce the message as of Satan, and stir up the sin-loving multitudes to revile and persecute those who proclaim it.

As the controversy extends into new fields, and the minds of the people are called to God's down-trodden law, Satan is astir. The power attending the message will only madden those who oppose it. The clergy will put forth almost superhuman efforts to shut away the light, lest it should shine upon their flocks. By every means at their command they will endeavor to suppress the discussion of these vital questions. The church appeals to the strong arm of civil power, and in this work, papists and Protestants unite. As the movement for Sunday enforcement becomes more bold and decided, the law will be invoked against commandment-keepers.—*GC* 606, 607.

[America] is fast filling up the cup of its iniquity. . . . How short-sighted is the policy that is being brought in by the rulers in the land to restore to the man of sin his lost ascendancy! They are manifesting wonderful zeal in taking this spurious sabbath under the care and protection of their legislatures; but they know not what they are doing. They are placing upon a false sabbath divine honors, and when this is fully done, persecution will break forth upon those who observe the Sabbath. . . . Then the commandment of men will be clothed with sacred garments, and will be pronounced holy.—*13MR* 69, 70; *Ms* 15, 1896.

Persecution will become progressively more severe

Men of position and reputation will join with the lawless and the vile to take counsel against the people of God. Wealth, genius, education, will combine to cover them with contempt. Persecuting rulers, ministers, and church members will conspire against them. With voice and pen, by boasts, threats, and ridicule, they will seek to overthrow their faith. By false representations and angry appeals they will stir up the passions of the people.—*5T* 450.

In the future, men claiming to be Christ's representatives will take a course similar to that followed by the priests and rulers in their treatment of Christ and the apostles. In the great crisis in which they are soon to pass, the faithful servants of God will encounter the same hardness of heart, the same cruel determination, the same unyielding hatred.—*AA* 431.

[Sabbath keepers] will be threatened with fines[60] and imprisonment, and some will be offered positions of influence, and other rewards and advantages, as inducements to renounce their faith. . . .

As the defenders of truth refuse to honor the Sunday-sabbath, some of them will be thrust into prison, some will be exiled,[61] some will be treated as slaves. . . .

As the storm approaches, a large class who have professed faith in the third angel's message, but have not been sanctified through obedience to the truth, abandon their position, and join the ranks of the opposition. . . . When Sabbath-keepers are brought before the courts to answer for their faith, these apostates are the most efficient agents of Satan to misrepresent and accuse them, and by false reports and insinuations to stir up the rulers against them. [{The}greatest trials {experienced by God's people}will come from those who have once advocated the truth, but who turn from it to the world, and trample it under their feet in hate and derision.][62] [{These apostates}will prove . . . {to be their}very worst persecutors.][63] [{They} will bear false witness against their [erstwhile] brethren, to secure their

---

60. "If the payment of a fine will deliver our brethren from the hands of these oppressors, let it be paid" (*UL* 40).

61. "There will come a time when there will be a great scattering . . . . Some . . . will be taken away to remote regions, but God will have a work for you [to do] there."—*5MR* 72, 73. This scattering obviously occurs *before* the close of probation, for God will have a work for the scattered ones to do when they arrive in these remote regions.

62. *RH*, 10 January 1888.

63. *RH*, 10 January 1888.

own safety. They will tell where their brethren are concealed, putting the wolves on their track. Christ has warned us of this, that we may not be surprised at the cruel, unnatural course pursued by friends and relatives."][64]

In this time of persecution the faith of the Lord's servants will be tried. They have faithfully given the warning, looking to God and to His word alone. God's Spirit, moving upon their hearts, has constrained them to speak. . . . Yet, when the storm of opposition and reproach bursts upon them, some, overwhelmed with consternation, will be ready to exclaim, "Had we foreseen the consequences of our words, we would have held our peace." They are hedged in with difficulties. Satan assails them with fierce temptations. The work which they have undertaken seems far beyond their ability to accomplish. They are threatened with destruction. The enthusiasm which animated them is gone; yet they cannot turn back. Then, feeling their utter helplessness, they flee to the Mighty One for strength. . . .

As the opposition rises to a fiercer height, the servants of God are again perplexed; for it seems to them that they have brought [on] the crisis. [{They} meet with perplexities that . . . {they} know not how to deal with.][65] But conscience and the word of God assure them that their course is right; and although the trials continue, they are strengthened to bear them. The contest grows closer and sharper, but their faith and courage rise with the emergency. . . .

So long as Jesus remains man's intercessor in the sanctuary above, the restraining influence of the Holy Spirit is felt by rulers and people. . . . The opposition of the enemies of truth will be restrained that the third angel's message may do its work. . . .

The angel who unites in the proclamation of the third angel's message is to lighten the whole earth with his glory. A work of world-wide extent and unwonted power is here foretold. . . .

The work will be similar to that of the day of Pentecost.—*GC* 607-611.

The progressive steps in the coming persecution

The Protestants of the United States will be foremost in stretching their hands across the gulf to grasp the hand of Spiritualism; they will reach over

---

64. *RH* 20 December 1898.
65. *8T* 254.

the abyss to clasp hands with the Roman power; and under the influence of this threefold union, this country will follow in the steps of Rome in trampling on the rights of conscience.—*GC* 588.

The time is coming when we cannot sell at any price. The decree will soon go forth prohibiting men to buy or sell of any man save him that hath the mark of the beast.—*5T* 152.

[Satan says in his strategy session,] "When death shall be made the penalty of violating our sabbath, then many who are now ranked with commandment-keepers will come over to our side."—*4SP* 338.

God's church will appear about to fall

I saw our people in great distress, weeping, and praying, pleading the sure promises of God, while the wicked were all around us, mocking us, and threatening to destroy us. They ridiculed our feebleness, they mocked at the smallness of our numbers, and taunted us with words calculated to cut deep. They charged us with taking an independent position from all the rest of the world. They had cut off our resources so that we could not buy nor sell, and referred to our abject poverty and stricken condition. They could not see how we could live without the world; we were dependent upon the world, and we must concede to the customs, practices, and laws of the world, or go out of it. If we were the only people in the world whom the Lord favored the appearances were awfully against us. They declared that they had the truth, that miracles were among them, that angels from heaven talked with them, and walked with them, that great power, and signs and wonders were performed among them, and [that] this was the Temporal Millennium, which they had been expecting so long. [They declared that] the whole world was converted and in harmony with the Sunday law, and this little feeble people stood out in defiance of the laws of the land, and the laws of God, and claimed to be the only ones right on the earth.[66]—*Mar* 209.

---

66. This statement seems to describe events that take place *before* probation closes, for this same letter goes on to say that "close about the throne were the martyrs. Among this number I saw the very ones who were so recently in such abject misery." Since, according to *The Great Controversy*, 634, none of God's people lose their lives after probation closes, it is most likely that these events occur *before* the close of probation.

The church will yet see troublous times. She will prophesy in sackcloth. But although she must meet heresies and persecutions, although she must battle with the infidel and the apostate, yet by the help of God she is bruising the head of Satan. The Lord will have a people as true as steel, and with faith as firm as the granite rock. They are to be His witnesses in the world, His instrumentalities to do a special, a glorious work[67] in the day of His preparation.—*4T* 594, 595.

The work which the church has failed to do in a time of peace and prosperity she will have to do in a terrible crisis under most discouraging, forbidding circumstances. The warnings that worldly conformity has silenced or withheld must be given under the fiercest opposition from enemies of the faith. And at that time the superficial, conservative class, whose influence has steadily retarded the progress of the work, will renounce the faith and stand with its avowed enemies, toward whom their sympathies have long been tending. These apostates will then manifest the most bitter enmity, doing all in their power to oppress and malign their former brethren and to excite indignation against them. . . . The members of the church will individually be tested and proved. They will be placed in circumstances where they will be forced to bear witness for the truth. Many will be called to speak before councils and in courts of justice, perhaps separately and alone.—*5T* 463.

The church may appear as about to fall, but it does not fall. It remains, while the sinners in Zion will be sifted out—the chaff separated from the precious wheat. This is a terrible ordeal, but nevertheless it must take place. None but those who have been overcoming by the blood of the Lamb and the word of their testimony will be found with the loyal and true. . . . The remnant that purify their souls by obeying the truth gather strength from the trying process, exhibiting the beauty of holiness amid the surrounding apostasy.—*7BC* 911.

---

67. Like the Jews of old, who were fond of looking forward to the glorious reign of the Messiah and overlooked the coming of Messiah as the Suffering Servant, Seventh-day Adventists are fond of looking forward to the glorious triumph of the third angel's message and seem to overlook the fact that before the message triumphs the church will go through terrible times. It is only after this shaking that the latter rain is poured out and the third angel's message triumphs. We must never forget that Satan, who instigated the murder of over 6 million Jews, does not love God's remnant people any more than he loved those Jews—in fact, he probably loves them less.

Only those who have withstood temptation in the strength of the Mighty One will be permitted to act a part in proclaiming . . . [the third angel's message] when it shall have swelled to the loud cry.—*HS* 155.

Satan, in cooperation with his angels and with evil men, will put forth every effort to gain the victory, and will appear to succeed. But from this conflict, truth and righteousness will come forth triumphant in victory.—*3SM* 393.

The great controversy between good and evil will increase in intensity to the very close of time. In all ages the wrath of Satan has been manifested against the church of Christ; and God has bestowed His grace and Spirit upon His people to strengthen them to stand against the power of the evil one. . . . But as the church approaches her final deliverance, Satan is to work with greater power. He comes down "having great wrath, because he knoweth that he hath but a short time." . . . And all the depths of satanic skill and subtlety acquired, all the cruelty developed, during these struggles of the ages, will be brought to bear against God's people in the final conflict. And in this time of peril the followers of Christ are to bear to the world the warning of the Lord's second advent.—*GC* ix, x.

Foretold, a time of severe persecution and martyrdom

The Christian world will learn what Romanism really is, when it is too late to escape the snare. She is silently growing into power. Her doctrines are exerting their influence in legislative halls, in the churches, and in the hearts of men. Throughout the land she is piling up her lofty and massive structures, in the secret recesses of which her former persecutions will be repeated.—*4SP* 397.

Protestants will work upon the rulers of the land [the United States] to make laws to restore the lost ascendancy of the man of sin, who sits in the temple of God, showing himself that he is God. The Roman Catholic principles will be taken under the care and protection of the state. This national apostasy will speedily be followed by national ruin. The protest of Bible truth will no longer be tolerated by those who have not made the law of God their rule of action. Then will the voice be heard from the graves of martyrs, represented by the souls which John saw slain for the word of God and the testimony of Jesus Christ which they held; then the prayer will ascend from every true child of God, "It is time for thee, Lord, to work, for they have made void thy law."—*TSA* 52.

By the decree enforcing the institution of the papacy in violation of the law of God, . . . [the United States] will disconnect herself fully from righteousness. . . . As the approach of the Roman armies was a sign to the disciples of the impending destruction of Jerusalem, so may this apostasy be a sign to us that the limit of God's forbearance is reached, that the measure of our nation's iniquity is full, and that the angel of mercy is about to take her flight, never to return. The people of God will then be plunged into those scenes of affliction and distress which prophets have described as the time of Jacob's trouble.[68] The cries of the faithful, persecuted ones ascend to heaven. And as the blood of Abel cried from the ground, there are voices also crying to God from martyrs' graves, from the sepulchers of the sea, from mountain caverns, from convent vaults.—*5T* 451.

The two armies will stand distinct and separate, and this distinction will be so marked that many who shall be convinced of truth will come on the side of God's commandment-keeping people. When this grand work is to take place in the battle, prior to the last closing conflict, many will be imprisoned, many will flee for their lives from cities and towns, and many will be martyrs[69] for Christ's sake in standing in defense of the truth.—*3SM* 397.

The severity of last-day persecution

There is no necessity for thinking that we cannot endure persecution; we shall have to go through terrible times.—*RH* 29 April 1890.

The persecutions of Protestants by Romanism, by which the religion of Jesus Christ was almost annihilated, will be more than rivaled when

---

68. Although the time of Jacob's trouble occurs *after* the close of probation, according to *Early Writings*, 36, 37, this statement suggests that there will be a time of Jacob's trouble for those who suffer martyrdom *after* America apostatizes nationally.

69. These martyrdoms obviously take place *before* the close of probation, for it will still be possible for those who choose to, to "come on the side of God's commandment-keeping people."

Protestantism and popery are combined. The scenes of the betrayal, the rejection, and the crucifixion of Christ have been re-enacted [during former times of persecution], and will again be re-enacted on an immense scale. People will be filled with the attributes of the enemy, and with them his delusions will have great power. . . .

The scenes enacted at the cross are being re-enacted. . . . We need not be surprised at anything that may take place now. We need not marvel at any developments of horror.—*RH* 30 January 1900.

I saw the souls of those who had been beheaded for the testimony of Jesus, and for the Word of God, those who did not worship the beast nor his image, and who did not receive his brand [or mark] upon their brow, or hand. And they lived and reigned with Christ for a thousand years.—Rev. 20:4, Montgomery.

It is the apostasy from truth that worketh in the children of disobedience to silence the voice of those who are calling them to obedience, and provoke the loyal to become disloyal as Cain tried to provoke Abel. A demoniacal spirit takes possession of men in our world. . . . Demon intelligence . . . will rend and destroy man formed in the divine similitude because . . . [man] cannot control the conscience of his brother and make him disloyal to God's holy law.—*UL* 285.

God promises spiritual power proportionate to trials in the coming crisis

Many will look away from present duties, present comfort and blessings, and be borrowing trouble in regard to the future crisis. This will be making a time of trouble beforehand, and we will receive no grace for any such anticipated troubles.—*3SM* 383, 384.

As we approach the end of earth's history we shall have increased power, proportionate to the trials to which we are subjected. We are not to keep ourselves in a state of worry and doubt.—*2MR* 329.

God does not give us the spirit of the martyrs to-day, for we have not come to the point of martyrdom. He is now testing us by smaller trials and crosses. And at times when it seems that the billows of temptation will go over our heads, let us remember that the eye of God is watching over us, and let us be willing to endure all the trials that he sees fit to send.—*HS* 233.

We must now be learning the lessons of faith if we would stand in that time of trouble which is coming upon all the world to try them who dwell upon the face of the earth. We must have the courage of heroes and the faith of martyrs.—*UL* 32.

Some of us may be brought to just as severe a test [as the worthies who refused to bow to the golden image]—will we obey the commandments of men or will we obey the commandments of God? . . . and, if He would have us be martyrs for the truth's sake, it may be the means of bringing many more into the truth.—*3SM* 420.

While we stand in defense of truth, let us not stand in defense of self, and [let us] not make a great ado because we are called to bear reproach and misrepresentation.—*RH* 10 January 1888.

Duration of the conflict

The last great conflict will be short, but terrible.—*GCDB* 2 March 1899.

Christ has shown us His battle plan

We have a living Saviour, and he has not left us in this world to fight the battles alone. No. But He has not flattered us [either]. . . . He tells us . . . "that whosoever killeth you will think that he doeth God service" (John 16:12). This is a terrible deception that comes upon the human mind. But here He has shown you the plan of the battle. He tells you what you are to meet: "We wrestle not against flesh and blood, but against principalities, against powers, against the rulers of the darkness of this world, against spiritual wickedness in high places" (Ephesians 6:12).—*Ms* 49, 1894.

The Lord has not concealed from His followers the plan of the battle. He has presented before His people the great conflict, and He has given them words of encouragement. He charges them not to enter into the battle without counting the cost, while He assures them that they do not fight alone, but that supernatural agencies will enable the weak, if they trust in Him, to become strong against the vast confederacy of evil arrayed against them. He points them to the universe of heaven, and assures them that holy beings are wrestling against principalities and powers and the rulers of the darkness of this world, and against spiritual wickedness in high places.

The children of God are cooperating with all the invisible host of light. And more than angels are in their ranks; the Holy Spirit, the representative of the Captain of the Lord's host, comes down to direct the battle.—*UL* 82.

The third angel's message will triumph gloriously

Servants of God, with their faces lighted up and shining with holy consecration, will hasten from place to place to proclaim the message from heaven. By thousands of voices, all over the earth, the warning will be given. [Men and women . . . so filled will they be by the Spirit of God that they will pass from country to country, from city to city, proclaiming the message of truth.][70] Miracles will be wrought, the sick will be healed, and signs and wonders will follow the believers. Satan also works with lying wonders, even bringing down fire from heaven in the sight of men. Thus the inhabitants of the earth will be brought to take their stand.—*GC* 612.

---

70. *UL* 16.

GOOD AND EVIL ANGELS AND SATAN'S PERSONATIONS

Superhuman forces in the great controversy

Our contest is not with human foes alone, but with the rulers, authorities, and cosmic powers of this dark world; that is, with the spirit-forces of evil[71] challenging us in the heavenly contest. So you must take on God's full armor, so as to be able to take a stand in the day when evil attacks you, and,

---

71. Behind the scenes of earthly affairs invisible forces are locked in mortal combat for the control of human minds. Unlike military engagements, neither side can make any headway in this warfare without the consent of the human agent. Angelic beings may be superior to human beings in knowledge and strength (2 Sam. 14:17; Ezek. 28:3), yet, strangely enough, human beings determine the outcome of the struggle. This is a basic principle governing the invisible, cosmic conflict between the forces of good and evil. Although human beings determine the outcome of the struggle, they cannot play off one side against the other indefinitely. Both sides seek total control—but with a difference. Because of our inborn propensity to evil, the forces of good can win only as we allow Christ total control of our lives. On the other hand, the forces of evil can win by gaining partial control. This means that by not choosing Christ's side, we are really choosing Satan's side.

At the present time the spirit beings, though real and capable of manifesting their presence, normally operate outside the field of sensory perception. But as the controversy intensifies, these forces, both good and evil, will be permitted greater freedom of action to manifest their presence visibly on the stage of earthly affairs.

after having completely finished the contest, to hold your own.—Eph. 6:12, 13, Charles B. Williams.

Are not all [God's] angels ministering spirits sent to serve those who will inherit salvation?—Heb. 1:14, NIV.

Satan can disguise himself to look like an angel of light!—2 Cor. 11:14, TEV.

There shall arise false Christs, and false prophets, and shall shew great signs and wonders; insomuch that, if it were possible, they shall deceive the very elect.—Matt. 24:24.

At the coming of the Lord there will be great activity on the part of Satan, in the form of all kinds of deceptive miracles, signs, and marvels, as well as of wicked attempts to delude—to the ruin of those who are on the path to destruction, because they have never received and loved the Truth to their own Salvation.—2 Thess. 2:9, 10, *The Twentieth Century New Testament*.

Spiritualism

Satan has long been preparing for his final effort to deceive the world. The foundation of his work was laid by the assurance given to Eve in Eden: "Ye shall not surely die."[72] "In the day ye eat thereof, then your eyes shall

---

72. The hallmark of religion is belief in a life after death, either because the soul is immortal or because there will be a resurrection of the dead. The adherents of some primitive religions worship no deity, yet they profess to hold communion with ancestral spirits.

With few exceptions, the Seventh-day Adventist Church being one of them, most religious people believe in the immortality of the soul or spirit, but spiritualists claim to be able to "prove" that this is true.

At present God is limiting the activities of angels, both good and evil. This restraint is linked to the degree of knowledge one has of spiritual things and the depth to which he has surrendered his will, either to Christ or Satan.

Scientific investigators like to control their experiments, but spirits are elusive entities. This means that human beings can never be certain that a spirit is submitting to scientific controls, even when it appears to be. Hence, as the coming crisis intensifies, evil angels may yet *appear* to submit to scientific "controls," while behind the scenes, they are flouting the rules and manipulating the evidence—*the better to deceive!*

be opened, and ye shall be as gods, knowing good and evil." [Genesis 3:4, 5.] Little by little he [Satan] has prepared the way for his masterpiece of deception in the development of Spiritualism. He has not yet reached the full accomplishment of his designs; but it will be reached in the last remnant of time. . . . Except those who are kept by the power of God, through faith in His word, the whole world will be swept into the ranks of this delusion.—*GC* 561, 562.

Spirit "proofs"

Many who refuse the message which the Lord sends them are seeking to find pegs on which to hang doubts. . . .

The day is just before us when Satan will answer the demand of these doubters and present numerous miracles to confirm the faith of all those who are seeking this kind of evidence.—*Ev* 594; *Lt* 4, 1889.

It is not difficult for the evil angels to represent both saints and sinners who have died, and make these representations visible to human eyes.[73] These manifestations will be more frequent, and developments of a more startling character will appear as we near the close of time.—*RH* 1 April 1875.

Satan-caused calamities and communications from the spirits

In accidents and calamities by sea and by land, in great conflagrations, in fierce tornadoes and terrific hail-storms, in tempests, floods, cyclones, tidal waves, and earthquakes, in every place and in a thousand forms, Satan is exercising his power. He sweeps away the ripening harvest, and famine and distress follow. He imparts to the air a deadly taint, and thousands perish by the pestilence. These visitations are to become more and more frequent and disastrous. . . .

---

73. Angels are normally invisible, existing outside of our ken and control. This means that they have an insurmountable advantage over us humans. It means we can never be sure of their true identity—*except as we compare what they teach or imply by their presence with the Word of God!* This means that when God's angels appear, what they say or imply by their presence always harmonizes with Bible truth, whereas evil angels may *seem* to agree with the Bible, but in time, *sometimes almost imperceptibly*, what they teach or imply leads away from Bible truth.

And then the great deceiver will persuade men that those who serve God are causing these evils. . . . It will be declared that men are offending God by the violation of the Sunday-sabbath. . . .

The miracle-working power manifested through spiritualism will exert its influence against those who choose to obey God rather than men. Communications from the spirits will declare that God has sent them to convince the rejecters of Sunday of their error, affirming that the laws of the land should be obeyed as the law of God. They will lament the great wickedness in the world, and second the testimony of religious teachers, that the degraded state of morals is caused by the desecration of Sunday. Great will be the indignation excited against all who refuse to accept their testimony.—*GC* 589-591.

Many will be confronted by the spirits of devils personating beloved relatives or friends,[74] and declaring the most dangerous heresies. These visitants will appeal to our tenderest sympathies, and will work miracles to sustain their pretensions. We must be prepared to withstand them with the Bible truth that the dead know not anything, and that they who thus appear are the spirits of devils.—*GC* 560.

The popular ministry cannot successfully resist spiritualism.[75] They have nothing wherewith to shield their flocks from its baleful influence. Much of the sad result of spiritualism will rest upon ministers of this age; for they have trampled the truth under their feet, and in its stead have preferred fables.—*1T* 344.

---

74. Evil spirits can only be defeated the same way that Jesus defeated the arch deceiver in the wilderness of temptation—*by using "the sword of the Spirit, which is the word of God"* (Eph. 6:17, emphasis supplied). No other weapon can be successful in this spiritual warfare. As Jesus repulsed Satan by quoting Scripture, so may we repel impersonating demons, but we must be wholly committed to God when we do this. This means that we must know what the Bible teaches about man's unconsciousness in death and the agency of evil spirits; for, "except those who are kept by the power of God, through faith in His word, the whole world will be swept into the ranks of" spiritualism (*GC* 562).

75. The main reason the popular ministry will not be able to resist the baleful effects of spiritualism successfully is because they reject the Bible teaching concerning the state of the dead and subscribe to the belief that the soul is immortal by nature.

Good and evil angels in human form in the closing conflict

Satanic agencies in human form will take part in this last great conflict to oppose the building up of the kingdom of God. And heavenly angels in human guise will be on the field of action. The two opposing parties will continue to exist till the closing up of the last great chapter in this world's history.—*RH* 5 August 1909.

Satan will use every opportunity to seduce men from their allegiance to God. He and the angels who fell with him will appear on the earth as men, seeking to deceive. God's angels, also, will appear as men, and will use every means in their power to defeat the purposes of the enemy. We, too, have a part to act.—*HFM* 66.

Evil angels in human form among Seventh-day Adventists

I have been shown that evil angels in the form of believers will work in our ranks to bring in a strong spirit of unbelief. Let not even this discourage you, but bring a true heart to the help of the Lord against the powers of satanic agencies.

These powers of evil will assemble in our meetings, not to receive a blessing, but to counterwork the influence of the Spirit of God. . . . Christ was the instructor in the assemblies of these angels before they fell from their high estate.—*3SM* 410.

The apostles, as personated by these lying spirits, are made to contradict what they wrote at the dictation of the Holy Spirit when on earth. They deny the divine origin of the Bible, and thus tear away the foundation of the Christian's hope and put out the light that reveals the way to heaven.—*GC* 557.

There will be seducing spirits and doctrines of devils in the midst of the church, and these evil influences will increase; but hold fast the beginning of your confidence firm unto the end.—*8MR* 345.

Evil angels in human form will talk with those who know the truth. Mingling with . . . [Christ's] hearers were [evil] angels in the form of men, making their suggestions, criticizing, misapplying, and misinterpreting the Saviour's words. . . .

In this time evil angels in the form of men will talk with those who know the truth. They will misinterpret and misconstrue the statements of the messengers of God.[76]—*3SM* 440, 411.

The forms of the dead will appear through the cunning device of Satan, and many will link up with the one who loveth and maketh a lie . . . Right among us some will turn away from the faith and give heed to seducing spirits and doctrines of devils, and by them the truth will be evil spoken of.—*BCL* 125.

Satan and his angels will appear on this earth as men, and will mingle with those, of whom God's Word says, "Some shall depart from the faith, giving heed to seducing spirits, and doctrines of devils."—*3SM* 409.

When these spiritualistic deceptions are revealed to be what they really are,—the secret workings of evil spirits,—those who have acted a part in them will become as men who have lost their minds.—*TDG* 312.

Satanic miracles

Wonderful scenes with which Satan will be closely connected, will soon take place. God's Word declares that Satan will work miracles. He will make people sick, and then will suddenly remove from them his satanic power. They will then be regarded as healed. These works of apparent healing will bring Seventh-day Adventists to the test.—*2SM* 53.

Some [Seventh-day Adventists] will be tempted to receive these wonders as from God. The sick will be healed before us. Miracles will be performed in our sight.[77]—*1T* 302.

---

76. Are we prepared for the "principalities and powers . . . of this dark world" to appear in our "assemblies"? We are told that they will "demoralize both men and women who, to all appearances, believe the truth" (*RH* 7 December 1897; cf *1T* 349).

77. The performance of a miracle is no proof that a wonder-worker is of God. "John [the Baptist] did no miracle," yet he was of God (John 10:40; cf. Luke 7:28). In the day of judgment many miracle-workers are represented as pleading, "Lord, have we not cast out demons in Your name? And done many wonders in Your name?" but the Lord says, "Depart from Me, you who practice lawlessness" (Matt. 7:22, 23, NKJV). The miracle workers to whom Christ says, "Depart from me," claim to be Christians (they call Him Lord) but what they teach is out of harmony with God's law. "To the law and *to* the testimony: if they speak not according to this word, *it is because* there is no light in them" (Isa. 8:20). The evidence that one is of God is revealed, not in the power to perform miracles, but by what one teaches and practices in comparison with what the Bible teaches.

If those through whom cures are performed, are disposed, on account of these manifestations, to excuse their neglect of the law of God and continue in disobedience, though they have power to any and every extent, it does not follow that they have the great power of God. On the contrary, it is the miracle-working power of the great deceiver.—*RH* 17 November 1885.

God's people are not the only ones who will have miracle-working power in the last days.[78] Satan and his agencies will work "with all power and signs and lying wonders, and with all deceivableness of unrighteousness in them that perish." It is not miracle-working power by which our faith is substantiated. We must rely upon the power of God. . . . His word, the Bible, is the foundation of our faith. Unless we plant our feet upon this foundation, unless we substantiate our faith "By every word that proceedeth out of the mouth of God," we shall be deceived by Satan when he comes in glory, claiming to be Christ.—*19MR* 54.

We are warned that in the last days . . . [Satan] will work with signs and lying wonders. And he will continue these wonders until the close of probation,[79] that he may point to them as evidence that he is an angel of light and not of darkness.—*RH* 17 November 1885.

Only those who have been diligent students of the Scriptures and who have received the love of the truth will be shielded from the powerful delusion that takes the world captive. By the Bible testimony these will detect the deceiver in his disguise. To all, the testing time will come. . . . Are

---

78. Just before probation closes God's people will perform miracles (*GC* 612), but it is not God's plan to convince the world of the truth of the third angel's message by means of miracles. "The way in which Christ worked was to preach the Word and to relieve suffering by miraculous works of healing. But . . . we cannot work now in this way; for Satan will exercise his power by working miracles" (*MM* 14). In the last days he "will counterfeit the miracles wrought" (*9T* 16). This is why under the false latter rain, which precedes the true latter rain (*GC* 464), Satan's agents taunt the saints that miracles are among them (*Mar* 209), implying that God's people do not have the power that they have to perform miracles.

79. The expression "he will continue these wonders until the close of probation" does not mean that Satan performs no more miracles after probation closes. This cannot be the case, for, according to *The Great Controversy,* 624, he "heals the diseases of the people" during the great time of trouble. Hence this expression means that he performs these wonders to prove that he is what he claims to be while he can still get people into coming over to his side, not that he will perform no more miracles after probation closes.

the people of God now so firmly established upon His word that they would not yield to the evidence of their senses? Would they, in such a crisis, cling to the Bible and the Bible only?—*GC* 625.

Good angels and God's people in the closing conflict

In this time, the last days of this earth's history, the people of God are to be invested with all power. Angels as well as men are to take part in the great closing work.—*Lt* 251, 1903.

When divine power is combined with human effort, the work will spread like fire in the stubble. God will employ agencies whose origin man will be unable to discern; angels[80] will do a work which men might have had the blessing of accomplishing, had they not neglected to answer the claims of God.—*RH* 16 December 1885.

It is impossible to give any idea of the experience of the people of God who will be alive on the earth when past woes and celestial glory will be blended.[81] They will walk in the light proceeding from the throne of God. By means of the angels there will be constant communication between heaven and earth.—*9T* 16.

As difficulties thicken about . . . [God's] people amid the perils of the last days, He sends His angels to walk all the way by our side.—*OHC* 317.

Our enemies will thrust us into prisons, but prison walls cannot cut off the communication between Christ and our souls. One who sees our every weakness, who is acquainted with every trial, is above all earthly powers; and angels can come to us in lonely cells, bringing light and peace from Heaven. The prison will be as a palace, for the rich in faith dwell there; and the gloomy walls will be lighted up with heavenly light.—*RH* 15 April 1884.

---

80. "Before the work is closed up and the sealing of God's people is finished, we shall receive the outpouring of the Spirit of God. Angels from heaven will be in our midst" (*1SM* 111). These statements help us to locate when in the sequence of coming events angels will assist in finishing God's work. They do this *when* the latter rain caps the climax of the loud cry. (See the next statement, *9T* 16.)

81. Celestial glory is blended with past woes (persecution) *during* the latter rain. (See *GC* 611, 612.)

Christ and His angels come to us in the form of human beings, and as we converse with them, light and grace and joy fill our hearts.—*9MR* 211.

We are to put on the whole armor of God. Having done all, we are to stand, meeting principalities and powers and spiritual wickedness in high places. And if we have on the heavenly armor, we shall find that the assaults of the enemy will not have power over us. Angels of God will be round about us to protect us.—*RH* 25 May 1905.

Satan brings all his powers to the assault in the last close conflict, and the endurance of the follower of Christ is taxed to the utmost. At times it seems that he must yield. But a word of prayer to the Lord Jesus goes like an arrow to the throne of God, and angels of God are sent to the field of battle. The tide is turned.—*HP* 297.

In the closing period of earth's history the Lord will work mightily in behalf of those who stand steadfastly for the right. . . . Angels that excel in strength will protect them.—*PK* 513.

Satanic personations before the close of probation

Satan . . . comes as an angel of light, and spreads his influence over the land by means of false reformations. The [Christian] churches are elated, and consider that God is working marvelously for them, when it is the work of another spirit.—*EW* 261.

Through spiritualism, Satan appears as a benefactor of the race, healing the diseases of the people, and professing to present a new and more exalted system of religious faith; but at the same time he works as a destroyer.—*GC* 589.

Satan will come in to deceive if possible the very elect. He claims to be Christ, and he is coming in, pretending to be the great medical missionary. He will cause fire to come down from heaven in the sight of men, to prove that he is God.—*RH* 14 April 1903.

Rebellion and apostasy are in the very air we breathe. We shall be affected by them unless we by faith hang our helpless souls upon Christ. If men are so easily misled now, how will they stand when Satan shall personate Christ, and work miracles? Who will be unmoved by his misrepresentations then—professing to be Christ when it is only Satan assuming the person of Christ, and apparently working the works of Christ?—*2SM* 394.

In this age antichrist will appear as the true Christ, and then the law of God will be fully made void in the nations of our world. Rebellion against God's holy law will be fully ripe. But the true leader of all this rebellion is Satan clothed as an angel of light. Men will be deceived and will exalt him to the place of God, and deify him. But Omnipotence will interpose, and to the apostate churches that unite in the exaltation of Satan,[82] the sentence will go forth, "Therefore shall her plagues[83] come in one day, death, and mourning, and famine; and she shall be utterly burned with fire: for strong is the Lord God who judgeth her."—*RH* 12 September 1893.

The conflict is to wax fiercer and fiercer. Satan will take the field and personate Christ. He will misrepresent, misapply, and pervert everything he possibly can, to deceive,[84] if possible, the very elect.—*TM* 411.

The time is coming when Satan will work miracles right in your sight, claiming that he is Christ; and if your feet are not firmly established upon the truth of God, then you will be led away from your foundation.—*RH* 3 April 1888.

Unless we plant our feet upon this foundation, unless we substantiate our faith "by every word that proceedeth out of the mouth of God," we shall be deceived by Satan when he comes in glory, claiming to be Christ.—*19MR* 54.

---

82. Although the papacy is "a form of Antichrist" (*RH* 31 July 1888), Satan, who "began" "rebellion . . . in heaven," is "antichrist" par excellence (*9T* 230; cf *UL* 135). This personation occurs before the close of probation; for it is *during* the latter rain that "celestial glory and a repetition of the persecutions of the past are blended" and "Satan, surrounded by evil angels . . . [claims] to be God" (*9T* 16); and Christ is God.
83. Because the plagues fall *after* the close of probation (*EW* 36, 37), it seems evident that this appearance of Satan occurs before the close of probation.
Sometimes Ellen White equates Satan's appearance as an angel of light with his personation of Christ. (See *6BC* 1106 and *5T* 698, quoted below.)
84. Notice that it does not say that this personation takes place at the climax of the conflict but when the conflict is waxing fiercer and fiercer. Satan's work of deceit and destruction "reaches its culmination in the time of trouble" after probation closes.

Before the close of time . . . [Satan] will perform actual miracles.[85] . . . Something more than mere impostures is brought to view in . . . [Rev. 13:14]. But there is a limit beyond which Satan cannot go, and here he calls deception to his aid and counterfeits the work which he has not power actually to perform. In the last days he will appear in such a manner as to make men believe him to be Christ come the second time into the world. He will indeed transform himself into an angel of light. But while he will bear the appearance of Christ in every particular, so far as mere appearance goes, it will deceive none but those who . . . are seeking to resist the truth.—*5T* 698.

It is impossible to give any idea of the experience of the people of God who shall be alive upon the earth when celestial glory and a repetition of the persecutions of the past are blended. They will walk in the light proceeding from the throne of God. By means of the angels there will be constant communication between heaven and earth. And Satan, surrounded by evil angels,[86] and claiming to be God, will work miracles of all kinds, to deceive, if possible, the very elect. God's people will not find their safety in working miracles, for Satan will counterfeit the miracles that will be wrought.—*9T* 16.

[Satan] will come personating Jesus Christ, working mighty miracles; and men will fall down and worship him as Jesus Christ. We shall be commanded to worship this being, whom the world will glorify as Christ.

---

85. Miracles are phenomena that appear to run contrary to the laws of nature as we understand them. When these phenomena can be explained, they cease to be miracles.
The working of "actual miracles" by Satan in the last days apparently means that God's people may not be able to explain why they are not of God. This should not surprise us. Evil spirits exist outside of our ken and control. This is what gives them such enormous power to deceive. Consequently, it is not surprising if in some cases we cannot explain why these miracles are satanic. When baffled by such phenomena, let us remember that, in the last analysis, our only security is reliance on "the power of God, through faith in His Word" (*GC* 562)—*not in our ability to unmask the deceptiveness of satanic miracles!*
86. The fact that Satan is surrounded by evil angels seems to suggest that he will try to imitate Christ's second coming as closely as possible. Although he will "not [be] permitted to counterfeit the manner of Christ's coming" (*GC* 625), he "is preparing his deceptions that in his last campaign against the people of God, they may not understand that it is he" (*4SG* 100, 101). How far he will be permitted to go, we do not know, but if one is to judge by the current interest in extraterrestrial life, Satan appears to be preparing the world for a counterfeit coming from outer space.

What shall we do?—Tell them that Christ has warned us against just such a foe, who is man's worst enemy,[87] yet who claims to be God.—*RH* 18 December 1888.

Disguised as an angel of light, . . . [Satan] will walk the earth as a wonder-worker. In beautiful language he will present lofty sentiments. Good words will be spoken by him, and good deeds performed. Christ will be personified, but on one point there will be a marked distinction. Satan will turn the people from the law of God. Notwithstanding this, so well will he counterfeit righteousness, that if it were possible, he would deceive the very elect. Crowned heads, presidents, rulers in high places, will bow to his false theories.—*RH* 17 August 1897.

Satan is determined to keep up the warfare to the end. Coming as an angel of light, claiming to be the Christ, he will deceive the world. But his triumph will be short. No storm or tempest can move those whose feet are planted on the principles of eternal truth. They will be able to stand in this time of almost universal apostasy.—*6BC* 1106.

Except those who are kept by the power of God, through faith in His word, the whole world will be swept into the ranks of . . . [spiritualism].—*GC* 562.

It is not miracle-working power by which our faith is substantiated. We must rely upon the power of God. We must stand upon His platform of eternal truth. His Word, the Bible, is the foundation of our faith. Unless we plant our feet upon this foundation, unless we substantiate our faith "By every word that proceedeth out of the mouth of God," we shall be deceived by Satan when he comes in glory, claiming to be Christ.—*19MR* 54.

---

87. This personation takes place *before* probation closes; for, *after* the probation closes, God's people dwell "in the most solitary places" (*4SP* 432), and there is no suggestion that they appeal to the wicked or point out their error. But even if this were not the case, telling those whose probation has closed that this being is Satan personating Christ would be gratutitous and would only enrage them. On the other hand, telling people that this is Satan, not Christ, *before* probation closes may lead some to turn away from the great deceiver and accept the third angel's message.

We can imagine the anger of those who reject the final warning when God's people say that this being, who "bear[s] the appearance of Christ in every particular" (*5T* 698), is not Christ but Satan masquerading as Christ. The saints will be accused of "blasphemy" (cf *EW* 86 and *2SG* 142) and of being worse than the Jews. "The Jews," they will say, "accused Christ of *having* a devil (John 7:20; 8:48), but you do worse; you accuse Christ of *being* the devil."

Satan's personation of Christ after the close of probation

As the second appearing of our Lord Jesus Christ draws near, satanic agencies are moved from beneath. Satan will not only[88] appear as a human being, but he will personate Jesus Christ; and the world who has rejected the truth will receive him as the Lord of lords and King of kings.—*RH* 14 April 1896.

One effort more, and then Satan's last device is employed. He hears the unceasing cry for Christ to come, for Christ to deliver . . . [His people]. This last strategy is to personate Christ, and make them think their prayers are answered.—*LDE* 165.

The wrath of Satan increases as his time grows short, and his work of deceit and destruction reaches its culmination in the time of trouble. God's long-suffering has ended. The world has rejected his mercy, despised his love, and trampled upon his law. The wicked have passed the boundary of their probation, and the Lord withdraws his protection, and leaves them to the mercy of the leader they have chosen.—*4SP* 441; cf *GC* 623.

As the crowning act in the great drama of deception, Satan himself will personate Christ. The church has long professed to look to the Saviour's advent as the consummation of her hopes. Now the great deceiver will make it appear that Christ has come. In different parts of the earth, Satan will manifest himself among men as a majestic being of dazzling brightness, resembling the description of the Son of God given by John in the Revelation. The glory that surrounds him is unsurpassed by anything that mortal eyes have yet beheld. The shout of triumph rings out upon the air, "Christ has come! Christ has come!" The people prostrate themselves in adoration before him, while he lifts up his hands, and pronounces a blessing upon them, as Christ blessed His disciples when He was upon the earth. His voice is soft and subdued, yet full of melody. In gentle, compassionate tones he presents some of the same gracious, heavenly truths which the Saviour uttered; he heals the diseases of the people, and then, in his assumed character of Christ, he

---

88. This is positive proof that Satan himself appears in the last days in more than one form.

claims to have changed the Sabbath to Sunday, and commands all to hallow the day which he has blessed. He declares that those who persist in keeping holy the seventh day are blaspheming his name by refusing to listen to his angels sent to them with light and truth. This is the strong, almost overmastering delusion.—*GC* 624.

Satan sees that he is about to lose his case. He cannot sweep in the whole world. He makes one last desperate effort to overcome the faithful by deception. He does this in personating Christ. He clothes himself with the garments of royalty which have been accurately described in the vision of John. [See Rev. 1:13-16; 19:11-16, and cf *GC* 624.] He has power to do this. He will appear to his deluded followers, the Christian world who received not the love of the truth but had pleasure in unrighteousness . . . as Christ coming the second time.

He proclaims himself Christ, and he is believed to be Christ, a beautiful, majestic being clothed with majesty and, with soft voice and pleasant words, with glory unsurpassed by anything their mortal eyes had yet beheld. Then his deceived, deluded followers set up a shout of victory, "Christ has come the second time! Christ has come! He has lifted up His hands just as He did when He was upon the earth, and blessed us." . . .

The saints look on with amazement. Will they also be deceived? Will they worship Satan? Angels of God are about them. A clear, firm, musical voice is heard, "Look up."

There is one object before the praying ones—the final and eternal salvation of their souls. This object was before them constantly—that immortal life was promised to those who endure unto the end. Oh, how earnest and fervent had been their desires. The [last] judgment and eternity were in view. Their eyes by faith were fixed on the blazing throne, before which the white-robed ones were to stand. This restrained them from the indulgence of sin.—*LDE* 164, 165.

Paul, in his second letter to the Thessalonians, points to the special working of Satan in Spiritualism as an event to take place immediately before the second advent of Christ. Speaking of Christ's second coming, he declares that it is "after the working of Satan with all power and signs and lying wonders" [2 Thess. 2:9].—*PP* 686.

CHAPTER Six

THE SEAL OF GOD, THE SEALING, AND THE 144,000

God's seal or mark

I saw four angels standing at the four corners of the earth, holding the four winds of the earth, that the wind should not blow on the earth, on the sea, or on any tree. Then I saw another angel ascending from the east, having the seal of the living God. And he cried with a loud voice to the four angels to whom it was granted to harm the earth and the sea, saying, "Do not harm the earth, the sea, or the trees till we have sealed the servants of our God on their foreheads." And I heard the number of those who were sealed. One hundred and forty-four thousand of all the tribes of the children of Israel were sealed.—Rev. 7:1-4, NKJV.

Suddenly six men came from the direction of the upper gate, which faces north, each with his battle-ax in his hand. One man among them was clothed with linen and had a writer's inkhorn at his side. They went in and stood beside the bronze altar. Now the glory of the God of Israel had gone up from the cherub, where it had been, to the threshold of the temple. And He called to the man clothed with linen, who had the writer's inkhorn at his side; and the Lord said to him, "Go through the midst of the city, through the midst of Jerusalem, and put a mark on the foreheads[89] of the men who sigh and cry over all the abominations that are done within it."—Ezek. 9:2-4, NKJV.

Do not grieve the Holy Spirit of God, by whom you were sealed for the day of redemption.—Eph. 4:30, NKJV.

Being sealed does not always involve the same test

I saw that she [Sister Hastings, who had recently died] was sealed and would come up at the voice of God and stand upon the earth, and would be with the 144,000.—*2SM* 263.

There are living upon our earth [in 1899] men who have passed the age of four score and ten. The natural results of old age are seen in their feebleness. But they believe God, and God loves them. The seal of God is upon them,[90] and they will be among the number of whom the Lord has said, "Blessed are the dead which die in the Lord."—*14MR* 57, 58.

The sealing that is followed by the close of probation

When the third angel's message closes, mercy no longer pleads for the guilty inhabitants of the earth. The people of God have accomplished their work. They have received "the latter rain," "the refreshing from the presence of the Lord," and they are prepared for the trying hour before them. Angels are

---

89. The "sealing of the servants of God [in Rev. 7:1-4] is the same that was shown to Ezekiel in vision" (*TM* 445).

90. Sealing does not mean the same thing every time it is used in the inspired writings, although the result—salvation—is the same in every case. Thus, the test Paul referred to in connection with the sealing of Ephesians 4:30: "Do not grieve the Holy Spirit of God, by whom you are sealed for the day of redemption" (NKJV) is not the same test that the 144,000 must pass through. In every age those who are sealed must pass the test of "present truth" (2 Pet. 1:12). In Noah's day present truth was acting upon the belief that a flood was coming. In New Testament times the test was belief that the crucified Christ, who was "to the Jews a stumbling block and to the Greeks foolishness" (1 Cor. 1:23, NKJV), was God manifested in the flesh. In the coming conflict the test will be the seventh-day Sabbath.

Unlike those who have been sealed and died, the 144,000 are called "the living saints" (*EW* 15). These are people who are "translated from the earth, from among the living" (*GC* 649). Hence, the 144,000 constitute a special group of the redeemed.

hastening to and fro in heaven. An angel returning from the earth announces that his work is done; the final test has been brought upon the world, and all who have proved themselves loyal to the divine precepts have received "the seal of the living God." Then Jesus ceases His intercession in the sanctuary above. He lifts His hands, and with a loud voice says, "It is done;" and all the angelic host lay off their crowns as He makes the solemn announcement: "He that is unjust, let him be unjust still: and he which is filthy, let him be filthy still: and he that is righteous, let him be righteous still: and He that is holy, let him be holy still." Every case has been decided for life or death. . . .

Satan will then plunge the inhabitants of the earth into one great, final trouble.—*GC* 613, 614.

Jesus is soon to step out from between God and man. The sealing will then be accomplished—finished up.—*5MR* 200; *Lt* 5, 1849.

Before the work is closed up and the sealing of God's people is finished, we shall receive the outpouring of the Spirit of God. Angels from heaven will be in our midst.—*1SM* 111.

The sealing that is followed by the shaking

Just as soon as the people of God are sealed in their foreheads—it is not any seal or mark that can be seen, but a settling into the truth, both intellectually and spiritually, so they cannot be moved—just as soon as God's people are sealed[91] and prepared for the shaking, it will come. Indeed, it has begun already; the judgments of God are now upon the land, to give us warning, that we may know what is coming.—*4BC* 1161; *Ms* 173, 1902.

Especially in the closing work of the church, in the sealing time of the one hundred and forty-four thousand,[92] who are to stand without fault

---

91. The sealing to which this statement refers cannot be the sealing that ends at the close of human probation (see *GC* 613), for this particular sealing is *followed* by the shaking or sifting.

92. Because there is a sealing that is followed by the shaking, and not the close of probation, "the sealing time of the one hundred forty-four thousand" obviously must end *earlier* than the sealing spoken of in *The Great Controversy,* 613, which ends at the close of probation. The next statement, *Testimonies for the Church,* 5:472-475, describes and locates when the special sealing of the 144,000 takes place.

before the throne of God, will they feel most deeply the wrongs of God's professed people.—*RH* 23 September 1873.

The remnant church will be brought into great trial and distress. Those who keep the commandments of God and the faith of Jesus will feel the ire of the dragon and his hosts. Satan numbers the world as his subjects, he has gained control of the apostate churches; but here is a little company that are resisting his supremacy. If he could blot them from the earth, his triumph would be complete. . . [I]n the near future he will stir up the wicked powers of earth to destroy the people of God. All will be required to render obedience to human edicts in violation of the divine law. Those who will be true to God and to duty will be menaced, denounced, and proscribed. They will "be betrayed both by parents, and brethren, and kinfolks, and friends."

Their only hope is in the mercy of God; their only defense will be prayer. . . [T]he remnant church, with brokenness of heart and earnest faith, will plead for pardon and deliverance through Jesus their Advocate. They are fully conscious of the sinfulness of their lives, they see their weakness and unworthiness, and as they look upon themselves they are ready to despair. The tempter stands by to accuse them . . . . He endeavors to affright . . . [them] with the thought that their case is hopeless, that the stain of their defilement will never be washed away. He hopes to so destroy their faith that they will yield to his temptations, turn from their allegiance to God, and receive the mark of the beast. . . .

But while the followers of Christ have sinned, they have not given themselves to the control of evil. They have put away their sins, and have sought the Lord in humility and contrition, and the divine Advocate pleads in their behalf.[93] . . .

The assaults of Satan are strong, his delusions are terrible; but the Lord's eye is upon His people. Their affliction is great, the flames of the furnace seem about to consume them; but Jesus will bring them forth as gold tried

---

93. Because "the divine Advocate [still] pleads in their behalf" and God's people are still "warning the wicked" and making "solemn appeals" to them, the events here described clearly take place *before* the close of probation. These events are *contemporaneous* with the description of God's "people in great distress, weeping, and praying, pleading the sure promises of God, while the wicked were all around . . . [them], mocking . . . [them], and threatening to destroy . . . [them]" (*Mar* 209), which definitely occurs *before* the close of probation.

in the fire. Their earthliness must be removed that the image of Christ may be perfectly reflected; unbelief must be overcome; faith, hope, and patience are to be developed.

The people of God are sighing and crying for the abominations done in the land.[94] With tears they warn the wicked of their danger in trampling upon the divine law, and with unutterable sorrow they humble themselves before the Lord on account of their own transgressions. The wicked mock their sorrow, ridicule their solemn appeals, and sneer at what they term their weakness. But the anguish and humiliation of God's people is unmistakable evidence that they are regaining the strength and nobility of character lost in consequence of sin. . . .

The faithful, praying ones are, as it were, shut in with God. They themselves know not how securely they are shielded. Urged on by Satan, the rulers of this world are seeking to destroy them; but could their eyes be opened, . . . they would see the angels of God encamped about them, by their brightness and glory holding in check the hosts of darkness.

As the people of God afflict their souls before Him, pleading for purity of heart, the command is given, "Take away the filthy garments" from them, and the encouraging words are spoken, "Behold, I have caused thine iniquity to pass from thee, and I will clothe thee with change of raiment." The spotless robe of Christ's righteousness is placed upon the tried, tempted, yet faithful children of God. The despised remnant are clothed in glorious apparel, nevermore to be defiled by the corruptions of the world. . . . They have resisted the wiles of the deceiver; they have not been turned from their loyalty by the dragon's roar. Now they are eternally secure from the tempter's devices. . . . While Satan was urging his accusations and seeking to destroy this company, holy angels, unseen, were passing to and fro, placing upon them the seal of the living God. These are they that stand upon Mount Zion with the Lamb, having the Father's name written in their foreheads. They sing the new song before the throne, that song which no man can learn save the hundred and forty-four thousand, which were redeemed from the earth.—*5T 472-475.*

---

94. *Testimonies for the Church,* 3:367, says that they sigh and cry for the abominations that are done "in the church."

Why . . . [are the 144,000] so specially singled out? Because they had to stand with a wonderful truth right before the whole world, and receive their opposition,[95] and while receiving this opposition they were to remember that they were sons and daughters of God, that they must have Christ formed within them the hope of glory.—*1SAT* 72, 73.

Only those who have withstood temptation in the strength of the Mighty One will be permitted to act a part in proclaiming . . . [the third angel's message], when it shall have swelled into the loud cry.[96]—*HS* 155.

Four mighty angels hold back the powers of this earth till the servants of God are sealed in their foreheads. The nations of the world are eager for conflict; but they are held in check by the angels. When this restraining power is removed, there will come a time of trouble and anguish. Deadly instruments of warfare will be invented. Vessels, with their living cargo, will be entombed in the great deep. All who have not the spirit of truth will unite under the leadership of satanic agencies. But they are to be kept under control till the time shall come for the great battle of Armageddon.—*7BC* 967; *Lt* 79, 1900.

Injurious influences controlled until the 144,000 are sealed

All injurious, discouraging influences are held in control by unseen angel hands until every one that works in the fear and love of God is sealed in his forehead.—*20MR* 217.

---

95. The reason the 144,000 are "specially singled out" is "because they had to stand with a wonderful truth right before the whole world, and receive their opposition" (*1SAT* 72, 73). This supports the conclusion that the 144,000 are the ones who are "permitted to act a part in proclaiming . . . [the third angel's message], when it shall have swelled into the loud cry" (*HS* 155). These are the people who are prepared for the "image to the beast . . . test," which "the people of God must have before they are sealed" (*EGW1888* 701). These are people who "have not been turned from their loyalty [to God] by the dragon's roar" (*PK* 591).
96. Notice that not all who profess to believe the third angel's message will be permitted to proclaim that message during the loud cry. Apparently those who are permitted to are those who have remained faithful in the face of the image-to-the-beast "test" (*7BC* 976). This test is applied when the decree is issued enforcing Sunday keeping in violation of Sabbath keeping *on pain of death.* It is this event that marks the time when "the sealing time of the 144,000" begins (*RH* 23 September 1873, quoted above). It appears, therefore, that the beginning of the sealing of the 144,000 marks the time when the investigative judgment passes from the dead to the living.

John sees the elements of nature—earthquake, tempest, and political strife—represented as being held by four angels. These winds are under control until God gives the word to let them go. There is the safety of God's church. The angels of God do His bidding, holding back the winds of the earth, that the winds should not blow on the earth, nor on the sea, nor on any tree, until the servants of God should be sealed in their foreheads. The mighty angel is seen ascending from the east (or sunrising). This mightiest of angels has in his hand the seal of the living God, or of Him who alone can give life, who can inscribe upon the foreheads the mark or inscription, to whom shall be granted immortality, eternal life. It is the voice of this highest angel that had authority to command the four angels to keep in check the four winds until this work was performed, and until he should give the summons to let them loose.

Those that overcome the world, the flesh, and the devil, will be the favored ones who shall receive the seal of the living God. Those whose hands are not clean, whose hearts are not pure, will not have the seal of the living God. Those who are planning sin and acting it will be passed by. Only those who, in their attitude before God, are filling the position of those who are repenting and confessing their sins in the great anti-typical day of atonement, will be recognized and marked as worthy of God's protection. The names of those who are steadfastly looking and waiting and watching for the appearing of their Saviour—more earnestly and wishfully than they who wait for the morning—will be numbered with those who are sealed. Those who, while having all the light of truth flashing upon their souls, should have works corresponding to their avowed faith, but are allured by sin, setting up idols in their hearts, corrupting their souls before God, and polluting those who unite with them in sin, will have their names blotted out of the book of life, and be left in midnight darkness, having no oil in their vessels with their lamps.—*TM* 444, 445.

Angels are belting the world, refusing Satan his claim to supremacy, made because of the vast multitude of his adherents. We hear not the voices, we see not with the natural sight the work of these angels, but their hands are linked about the world, and with sleepless vigilance they are keeping the armies of Satan at bay till the sealing of God's people shall be accomplished.—*7BC* 967; *Lt* 79, 1900.

Mark this point with care: Those who receive the pure mark of truth, wrought in them by the power of the Holy Ghost, . . . are those "that sigh and that cry for all the abominations that be done" in the church.—*3T* 267.

The four winds are held in check until the remnant are sealed

I saw an angel with a commission from Jesus, swiftly flying to the four angels who had a work to do on the earth, . . . crying with a loud voice, "Hold! Hold! Hold! Hold! until the servants of God are sealed in their foreheads." I asked my accompanying angel the meaning of what I heard, and what the four angels were about to do. He said to me that . . . the four angels had power from God to hold the four winds, and that they were about to let them go; but while their hands were loosening, and the four winds were about to blow, . . . Jesus gazed on the remnant[97] that were not sealed. . . . Then another angel was commissioned to fly swiftly to the four angels, and bid them hold, until the servants of God were sealed with the seal of the living God in their foreheads.—*EW* 38.

Four mighty angels are still holding the four winds of the earth. Terrible destruction is forbidden to come in full. The accidents by land and by sea; the loss of life, steadily increasing, by storm, by tempest, by railroad disaster, by conflagration; the terrible floods, the earthquakes, and the winds will be the stirring up of the nations to one deadly combat, while the angels hold the four winds, forbidding the terrible power of Satan to be exercised in its fury until the servants of God are sealed in their foreheads.—*RH* 7 June 1887.

The seal of God for the last days

What is the seal of the living God, which is placed in the foreheads of His people? It is a mark which angels,[98] but not human eyes, can read; for the destroying angel must see this mark of redemption.—*7BC* 968.

---

97. The angels holding the four winds begin to loosen them (*EW* 38) *before* the sealing of "the remnant," hence these people are not those who are sealed "in the sealing time of the 144,000" (*3T* 266). Notice that *before* letting the winds go, the angel from heaven commands the four angels to hold the winds until the sealing of "the remnant" is completed. This sealing ends with the close of probation (*GC* 613).

98. It is apparent that only God's angels can discern this mark; for, during the great time of trouble *after* probation has closed, Satan "sees that holy angels are guarding . . . [God's people] and he *infers* that their sins have been pardoned; but he does not *know* that their cases have been decided in the sanctuary above" (*GC* 618). Therefore, not only humans, but also evil angels, cannot read this mark.

The Sabbath will be the great test of loyalty; for it is the point of truth especially controverted. When the final test shall be brought to bear upon men, then the line of distinction will be drawn between those who serve God and those who serve Him not. While the observance of the false sabbath in compliance with the law of the state, contrary to the fourth commandment, will be an avowal of allegiance to a power that is in opposition to God, the keeping of the true Sabbath, in obedience to God's law, is an evidence of loyalty to the Creator. While one class, by accepting the sign of submission to earthly powers, receive the mark of the beast, the other, choosing the token of allegiance to divine authority, receive the seal of God.—*GC* 605.

The Sabbath is not introduced as a new institution but as having been founded at creation. It is to be remembered and observed as the memorial of the Creator's work. Pointing to God as the maker of the heavens and the earth, it distinguishes the true God from all false gods. All who keep the seventh day, signify by this act that they are worshipers of Jehovah. Thus the Sabbath is the sign of man's allegiance to God as long as there are any upon the earth to serve him. The fourth commandment is the only one of all the ten in which are found both the name and the title of the Lawgiver. It is the only one that shows by whose authority the law is given. Thus it contains the seal of God.—*PP* 307.

The seal of God's law is found in the fourth commandment. This only, of all the ten, brings to view both the name and the title of the Lawgiver. It declares Him to be the Creator of the heavens and the earth, and thus shows His claim to reverence and worship above all others. Aside from this precept, there is nothing in the decalogue to show by whose authority the law is given. When the Sabbath was changed by the papal power, the seal was taken from the law. The disciples of Jesus are called upon to restore it, by exalting the Sabbath of the fourth commandment to its rightful position as the Creator's memorial and the sign of His authority.—*GC* 452.

The Sabbath of the fourth commandment is the seal of the living God. It points to God as the Creator, and is the sign of His rightful authority over the beings He has made. Those who obey this law will bear the seal of God, for He has set apart this day as a sign of loyalty between Himself and His people.—*ST* 22 March 1910.

Those who would have the seal of God in their foreheads must keep the Sabbath of the fourth commandment. This is what distinguishes them from the disloyal, who have accepted a man-made institution in the place of the true Sabbath. The observance of God's rest day is the mark of distinction between him that serveth God and him that serveth Him not.—*7BC* 970.

Who receive the seal of God

The image of the beast will be formed before probation closes; for it is to be the great test for the people of God, by which their eternal destiny will be decided. . . . This is the test that the people of God must have before they are sealed. All who prove their loyalty to God by observing His law, and refusing to accept a spurious sabbath, . . . will receive the seal of the living God.—*15MR* 15.

The seal of the living God is placed upon those who conscientiously keep the Sabbath of the Lord.—*RH* 13 July 1897.

If we receive the image of God, if our souls are cleansed from every moral defilement, the seal of God will be placed upon our foreheads, and we shall be prepared for the closing scenes of this earth's history.—*SD* 342.

Are we striving with all our God-given powers to reach the measure of the stature of men and women in Christ? Are we seeking for His fullness, ever reaching higher and higher,[99] trying to attain to the perfection of His character? When God's servants reach this point, they will be sealed in their foreheads.—*3SM* 427.

In a little while every one who is a child of God will have His seal placed upon him. O that it may be placed upon our foreheads! Who can endure the

---

99. What is described here is a preparatory work accomplished under the early rain. "Reaching higher and higher" simply means making a deeper and deeper commitment to follow God's will as He, through His Spirit, brings to mind things that are out of harmony with His will and these things are overcome by His grace.

thought of being passed by when the angel goes forth to seal the servants of God in their foreheads?—*RH* 28 May 1889.

The message of the renewing power of God's grace will be carried to every country and clime, until the truth shall belt the world. Of the number of them that shall be sealed will be those who have come from every nation and kindred and tongue and people.—*CT* 532.

Satan . . . knows that his time is short and that the sealing of the saints will place them beyond his power.—*8MR* 220.

Who do not receive the seal of God

Those who are uniting with the world are receiving the worldly mold and preparing for the mark of the beast. Those who are distrustful of self, who are humbling themselves before God and purifying their souls by obeying the truth—these are receiving the heavenly mold and preparing for the seal of God in their foreheads. When the decree goes forth and the stamp is impressed, their character will remain pure and spotless for eternity. Now is the time to prepare. The seal of God will never be placed upon the forehead of an impure man or woman. It will never be placed upon the forehead of the ambitious, world-loving man or woman. It will never be placed upon the forehead of men or women of false tongues or deceitful hearts. All who receive the seal must be without spot before God—candidates for heaven.—*FLB* 288.

If the light of truth has been presented to you, revealing the Sabbath of the fourth commandment, and showing that there is no foundation in the Word of God for Sunday observance, and yet you still cling to the false sabbath, refusing to keep holy the Sabbath which God calls "My holy day," you receive the mark of the beast. When does this take place? When you obey the decree that commands you to cease from labor on Sunday and worship God, while you know that there is not a word in the Bible showing Sunday to be other than a common working day, you consent to receive the mark of the beast, and refuse the seal of God.—*RH* 13 July 1897.

Not all who profess to keep the Sabbath will be sealed. There are many even among those who teach the truth to others who will not receive the seal of God in their foreheads. They had the light of truth, they knew their Master's will, they understood every point of our faith, but they had not corresponding works.—*5T* 213, 214.

Those who have been members of the same family are separated. A mark is placed upon the righteous. "They shall be Mine, saith the Lord of hosts, in that day when I make up My jewels; and I will spare them, as a man spareth his own son that serveth him [Mal. 3:17]." Those who have been obedient to God's commandments will unite with the company of the saints in light: they shall enter in through the gates into the city, and have right to the tree of life. The one shall be taken. His name shall stand in the book of life, while those with whom he associated shall have the mark of eternal separation from God.—*TM* 234, 235.

Probation of Adventists closes before the probation of the world

Had the people of God believed Him and been doers of His word, had they kept His commandments, the angel would not have come flying through heaven with the message to the four angels that were to let loose the winds that they should blow upon the earth crying, "Hold, hold the four winds that they blow not upon the earth until I have sealed the servants of God in their foreheads."[100] But because the people are disobedient, unthankful, unholy, as were ancient Israel, time is prolonged that all may hear the last message of mercy proclaimed with a loud voice. The Lord's work has been hindered, the sealing time delayed. Many have not heard the truth. But the Lord will give them a chance to hear and be converted, and the great work of God will go forward.—*15MR* 292.

O that the people might know the time of their visitation! There are many who have not yet heard the testing truth for this time. There are many with whom the Spirit of God is striving. The time of God's destructive judgments is the time of mercy for those who have had no opportunity

---

100. The sealing referred to here is the general sealing which is completed at the close of probation. Observe that these are not people who have heard the last message of mercy before; they are people who have never heard it up to this time.

[until then] to learn what is truth. Tenderly will the Lord look upon them. His heart of mercy is touched; His hand is still stretched out to save, while the door is closed to those who would not enter.[101]—*9T* 97.

God's Spirit will pass by those who have had their day of test and opportunity, but who have not distinguished the voice of God or appreciated the movings of His Spirit. Then thousands in the eleventh hour will see and acknowledge the truth. "Behold the days come, saith the Lord, that the plowman shall overtake the reaper, and the treader of grapes him that soweth seed" (Amos 9:13). These conversions to truth will be made with a rapidity that will surprise the church, and God's name alone will be glorified.[102]—*2SM* 16.

What it means to be sealed

The sealing is a pledge from God of perfect security to His chosen ones (Ex. 31:13-17). Sealing indicates [that] you are God's chosen. He has appropriated you to Himself.—*15MR* 225.

Just as soon as the people of God are sealed in their foreheads—it is not any seal or mark that can be seen, but a settling into the truth, both intellectually and spiritually, so they cannot be moved—just as soon as God's people are sealed and prepared for the shaking, it will come.—*4BC* 1161.

The bottles of God's wrath cannot be poured out to destroy the wicked and their works until all the people of God have been judged, and the cases of the living as well as the dead are decided. And even after the saints are

---

101. *This Day With God,* 163, reads identically, except that it adds, "Large numbers will be admitted who in these last days hear the truth for the first time." This latter addition locates these events at the time when the third angel's message goes forth under the latter rain. (See *GC* 612.)
Among those who will be saved during the final warning, "when self-denying efforts . . . [are] put forth to save the lost," will doubtless be "many who have strayed from the fold." These "will come back to follow the great shepherd" (*6T* 401) before it is too late. While this holds out hope for those who have backslidden loved ones, it should encourage no backslider to put off his calling and election in the expectation of returning to the fold at the last minute.
102. If these accessions were to occur while the church is in a Laodicean state, it would tend to take the glory to itself rather than giving the glory to God.

sealed with the seal of the living God, His elect will have trials individually.—*TM* 446.

The deliverance of the 144,000

I saw that the four angels would hold the four winds until Jesus' work was done in the sanctuary, and then will come the seven last plagues. These plagues enraged the wicked against the righteous; they thought that we had brought the judgments of God upon them, and that if they could rid the earth of us, the plagues would then be stayed. A decree went forth to slay the saints, which caused them to cry day and night for deliverance. This was the time of Jacob's trouble. Then all the saints cried out with anguish of spirit, and were delivered by the voice of God. The 144,000 triumphed.—*EW* 36, 37.

Soon we heard the voice of God like many waters, which gave us the day and hour of Jesus' coming. The living saints,[103] 144,000 in number,[104] knew and understood the voice, while the wicked thought it was thunder and an earthquake.—*EW* 15.

As God spoke the day and the hour of Jesus' coming, and delivered the everlasting covenant to His people, He spoke one sentence, and then paused, while the words were rolling through the earth. The Israel of God stood with their eyes fixed upward, listening to the words as they came from the mouth of Jehovah, and rolled through the earth like peals of loudest thunder. It was awfully solemn. And at the end of every sentence the saints shouted, "Glory! Alleluia!" Their countenances were lighted up with the glory of God; and they shone with the glory, as did the face of Moses when he came down from Sinai. The wicked could not look on them for the glory. And when the never-ending blessing was pronounced on those who had honored God in keeping His Sabbath

---

103. "The living saints." *The Great Controversy,* 649, refers to these people as "having been trans-lated from the earth, from among the living," hence, these are saints of the last generation. These are people who never die but are sealed and live until the Second Coming.
104. It is not clear whether "the living saints, 144,000 in number," means that literally only 144,000 will live through the great time of trouble or whether the number is symbolic. Perhaps this lack of clarity is by divine design. Hopefully the number is symbolic and includes a much larger number of individuals than 144,000.

holy, there was a mighty shout of victory over the beast and over his image.—*EW* 34.

Jesus' silver trumpet sounded, as He descended on the cloud, wrapped in flames of fire. He gazed on the graves of the sleeping saints, then raised His eyes and hands to heaven, and cried, "Awake! awake! awake! ye that sleep in the dust, and arise." Then there was a mighty earthquake. The graves opened, and the dead came up clothed with immortality. The 144,000 shouted, "Alleluia!" as they recognized their friends who had been torn from them by death.—*EW* 16.

The trials and triumph of the 144,000

Upon the crystal sea before the throne, that sea of glass as it were mingled with fire,—so resplendent is it with the glory of God,—are gathered the company that have "gotten the victory over the beast, and over his image, and over his mark, and over the number of his name." With the Lamb upon Mount Zion, "having the harps of God," they stand, the hundred and forty and four thousand[105] that were redeemed from among men. . . . And they sing "a new song" before the throne, a song which no man can learn save the hundred and forty and four thousand . . . for it is the song of their experience,—an experience such as no other company have ever had. "These are they which follow the Lamb whithersoever He goeth." These, having been translated from the earth, from among the living, are counted as "the firstfruits unto God and to the Lamb." "These are they which came out of great tribulation;" they have passed through the time of trouble such as never was since there was a nation; they have endured the anguish of the time of Jacob's trouble; they have stood without an intercessor through the final outpouring of God's judgments. But they have been delivered.—*GC* 648, 649.

Who the 144,000 Are Is Not Revealed

I have no light on the subject [of who will constitute the 144,000].—Ellen White, quoted in a letter by C. C. Crisler to E. E.

---

105. Whether literal or symbolic, the 144,000 constitute a special group of God's last-day people, for no other previous group will have gone through the experience they go through.

Andross, 18 December 1914. White Estate DF No. 164.

Letters will come asking questions in regard to the sealing of the people of God, who will be sealed, how many, and other prying questions. I think we must tell them to read and speak of the things that are plainly revealed. We have encouragement in the Word that if we walk humbly with God, we shall receive instruction. But prying curiosity is not to be encouraged.—*7BC* 918.

It is not . . . [God's] will that . . . [His people] shall get into controversy over questions which will not help them spiritually, such as, Who is to compose the hundred and forty-four thousand? This those who are the elect of God will in a short time know without question.[106]—*1SM* 174.

Let us strive with all the power that God has given us to be among the hundred and forty-four thousand.—*RH* 9 March 1905.

---

106. The 144,000 are those who in this life have learned to "follow the Lamb wherever He goes" (Rev. 14:4, NKJV). "The vision of . . . [Rev. 14:1-4] pictures them as standing on Mount Zion, girt for holy service, clothed with white linen, which is the righteousness of saints. But *those who follow the Lamb in heaven must first have followed Him here on earth*" (*AA* 591).

Being sensitive to the Holy Spirit's promptings, and obeying these promptings as soon as we become aware of them, is something that every Christian can learn and should learn *now* by God's grace—and His "grace is sufficient" for every trial and temptation (2 Cor. 12:9).

We should ever remember that there is nothing God intends to do for the 144,000 that He is unwilling to do for us now.

THE SIFTING OR SHAKING AND THE OMEGA OF APOSTASY

Predicted shakings and apostasies

"Yet once more," indicates the removal of those things that are being shaken, . . . that the things which cannot be shaken may remain. Therefore, since we are receiving a kingdom which cannot be shaken, let us have grace, by which we may serve God acceptably with reverence and godly fear—Heb. 12:27, 28, NKJV.

I will shake the house of Israel among all the nations as grain is shaken in a sieve, but not a kernel will fall to the ground.—Amos 9:9, NIV.

[The] man of sin . . . will completely fool those who are on their way to hell because they have said "no" to the Truth; they have refused to believe it and love it, and let it save them, so God will allow them to believe lies with all their hearts, and all of them will be justly judged for believing falsehood, refusing the Truth, and enjoying their sins.—2 Thess. 2:9-11, TLB.

The early shaking and the eschatological shaking

The mighty shaking has commenced, and will go on,[107] and all will be shaken out who are not willing to take a bold and unyielding stand for the truth, and sacrifice for God and his cause.—*PT* 1 April 1850.

The days of purification of the church are hastening on apace. God will have a people pure and true. In the mighty sifting soon to take place we shall be better able to measure the strength of Israel. The signs reveal that the time is near when the Lord will manifest that His fan is in His hand, and He will thoroughly purge His floor.—*5T* 80.

Just as soon as God's people are sealed and prepared for the shaking, it will come.—*4BC* 1161.

[Those who apostatized] fell all the way along the path one after another, until we heard the voice of God[108] like the sound of many waters, . . . which gave us the day and hour of Jesus' coming.—*WLF* 14.

The chaff must be removed, and it will require close work to separate the chaff from the kernels of grain. God's discerning eye will detect the smallest particle of chaff, and yet he will not cause to fall upon the ground the least kernel of grain.—*RH* 26 November 1861.

Nothing short of real, genuine faith will survive the strain that will come upon every soul of man in these last days to test and try him. God must be our refuge; we cannot trust in form, profession, ceremony, or position, or think that because we have a name to live, we shall be able to stand in the

---

107. There was a shaking that began in the early days of the Advent movement and is still going on. But this is not the shaking with which this study is primarily concerned. The shaking with which this study is concerned is yet future.

108. An individual's eternal destiny is fixed *before* the close of probation, at the time he is sealed. This means that those who fell off the path *after* the close of probation are only apparent apostates. The destiny of these individuals was fixed *before* probation closed, but it did not become apparent until *after* it had closed. "Not all who profess to keep the Sabbath will be sealed" (*5T* 213). It is these unsealed ones, who may even be enduring persecution for keeping the Sabbath, "who come up to the last fearful conflict unprepared, . . . [and who,] in their despair, confess their sins in words of burning anguish, while the wicked exult over their distress" (*GC* 620).

day of trial. Everything that can be shaken will be shaken, and those things that cannot be shaken by the deceptions and delusions of these last days, will remain. Rivet the soul to the eternal Rock; for in Christ alone there will be safety.—*YI* 3 August 1893.

A representational view of the shaking

I saw some, with strong faith and agonizing cries, pleading with God. Their countenances were pale and marked with deep anxiety, expressive of their internal struggle. Firmness and great earnestness was expressed in their countenances; large drops of perspiration fell from their foreheads. Now and then their faces would light up with the marks of God's approbation, and again the same solemn, earnest, anxious look would settle upon them.

Evil angels crowded around, pressing darkness upon them to shut out Jesus from their view, that their eyes might be drawn to the darkness that surrounded them, and thus they be led to distrust God and murmur against Him. Their only safety was in keeping their eyes directed upward. Angels of God had charge over His people, and as the poisonous atmosphere of evil angels was pressed around these anxious ones, the heavenly angels were continually wafting their wings over them to scatter the thick darkness.

As the praying ones continued their earnest cries, at times a ray of light from Jesus came to them, to encourage their hearts and light up their countenances. Some, I saw, did not participate in this work of agonizing and pleading. They seemed indifferent and careless. They were not resisting the darkness around them, and it shut them in like a thick cloud. The angels of God left these and went to the aid of the earnest, praying ones. I saw angels of God hasten to the assistance of all who were struggling with all their power to resist the evil angels and trying to help themselves by calling upon God with perseverance. But His angels left those who made no effort to help themselves, and I lost sight of them.

I asked the meaning of the shaking I had seen and was shown that it would be caused by the straight testimony called forth by the counsel of the True Witness to the Laodiceans. This will have its effect upon the heart of the receiver, and will lead him to exalt the standard and pour forth the straight truth. Some will not bear this straight testimony. They will rise up against it, and this is what will cause a shaking among God's people. . . .

My attention was then turned to the company I had seen, who were mightily shaken. I was shown those whom I had before seen weeping and praying in agony of spirit. The company of guardian angels around them had been doubled, and they were clothed with an armor from their head to their feet. They moved in exact order, like a company of soldiers. Their countenances expressed the severe conflict which they had endured, the agonizing struggle they had passed through. Yet their features, marked with severe internal anguish, now shone with the light and glory of heaven. They had obtained the victory, and it called forth from them the deepest gratitude and holy, sacred joy.

The numbers of this company had lessened. Some had been shaken out and left by the way. The careless and indifferent, who did not join with those who prized victory and salvation enough to perseveringly plead and agonize for it, did not obtain it, and they were left behind in darkness, and their places were immediately filled by others taking hold of the truth and coming into the ranks. Evil angels still pressed around them, but could have no power over them.

I heard those clothed with the armor speak forth the truth with great power. It had effect. Many had been bound; some wives by their husbands, and some children by their parents. The honest who had been prevented from hearing the truth now eagerly laid hold upon it. All fear of their relatives was gone, and the truth alone was exalted to them. They had been hungering and thirsting for truth; it was dearer and more precious than life. I asked what had made this great change. An angel answered, "It is the latter rain, the refreshing from the presence of the Lord, the loud cry of the third angel."—*EW* 269-271.

Persecution brings about the sifting or shaking

All the policy in the world cannot save us from a terrible sifting, and all the efforts made with high authorities will not lift from us the scourging of God, just because sin is cherished. . . .

All the struggles to carry our appeals to the highest authorities in our land, however earnest and strong and eloquent may be the pleas in our favor, will not bring about that which we desire, unless the Lord works by His Holy Spirit in the hearts of those who claim to believe the truth.[109]—*3SM* 385.

The Word of God plainly declares that His law is to be scorned, trampled upon, by the world; there will be an extraordinary prevalence of iniquity. The professed Protestant world will form a confederacy with the man of sin, and the church and the world will be in corrupt harmony.

Here the great crisis is coming upon the world. The Scriptures teach that popery is to regain its lost supremacy, and that the fires of persecution will be rekindled through the time-serving concessions of the so-called Protestant world. In this time of peril we can stand only as we have the truth and the power of God. . . .

In the absence of persecution, there have drifted into our ranks some who appear sound, and their Christianity unquestionable, but who, if persecution should arise, would go out from us.[110] . . . When the law of God is made void the church will be sifted by fiery trials, and a larger proportion than we now anticipate will give heed to seducing spirits and doctrines of devils.—*GCDB* 13 April 1891.

The shaking of God blows away multitudes like dry leaves. Prosperity multiplies a mass of professors. Adversity purges them out of the church.—*4T* 89.

The majority will forsake us

Many who claim to believe the truth will change their opinions in times of peril, and will take the side of the transgressors of God's law in order to escape persecution.—*EGW1888* 166.

---

109. We "who have been warned of the events before . . . [us] are not to sit in calm expectation of the coming storm, comforting . . . [ourselves] that the Lord will shelter His faithful ones in the day of trouble" (*5T* 452). Rather, we should do all we can to oppose Sunday legislation, even though we know that eventually the United States and in time all nations will substitute Sunday for the Sabbath. Our reason for opposing Sunday laws is because our opposition puts us, or keeps us, on the right side of the issue in the coming conflict. It is not because we think we can hold off Sunday legislation indefinitely.

110. We must not be paranoid, but on the other hand, let us not be naive to the possibility that Satan's "plants" have "drifted into our ranks." In the future these will act as agents provocateurs—individuals who will do shameful and outrageous things. We are warned that our enemies *"will demoralize both men and women who, to all appearances, believe the truth"* (*RH* 7 December 1897, emphasis supplied). When this happens, it will be a temptation even for the loyal to say "This isn't my church."

An apostate church will unite with the powers of earth and hell to place upon the forehead or in the hand, the mark of the beast, and prevail upon the children of God to worship the beast and his image. They will seek to compel them to renounce their allegiance to God's law, and yield homage to the papacy. Then will come the times which will try men's souls; for the confederacy of apostasy will demand that the loyal subjects of God shall renounce the law of Jehovah, and repudiate the truth of his word. Then will the gold be separated from the dross, and it will be made apparent who are the godly, who are loyal and true, and who are the disloyal, the dross and the tinsel. What clouds of chaff will then be borne away by the fan of God! Where now our eyes can discover only rich floors of wheat, will be chaff blown away with the fan of God. Every one who is not centered in Christ will fail to stand the test and ordeal of that day. While those who are clothed with Christ's righteousness will stand firm to truth and duty, those who have trusted in their own righteousness will be ranged under the black banner of the prince of darkness.—*RH* 8 November 1892.

Classes of Adventists that will leave the church

Let opposition arise, let bigotry and intolerance again bear sway, let persecution be kindled, and the half-hearted and hypocritical will waver and yield the faith; but the true Christian will stand firm as a rock, his faith stronger, his hope brighter, than in days of prosperity.—*GC* 602.

The time is not far distant when the test will come to every soul. The observance of the false sabbath will be urged upon us. The contest will be between the commandments of God and the commandments of men. Those who step by step have yielded to worldly demands and conformed to worldly customs will then yield to the powers that be, rather than subject themselves to derision, insult, threatened imprisonment and death. At this time the gold will be separated from the dross. True godliness will be clearly distinguished from the appearance and tinsel of it. Many a star that we have admired for its brilliance will then go out in darkness. Those who have assumed the ornaments of the sanctuary, but are not clothed with Christ's righteousness, will then appear in the shame of their own nakedness.—*RH* 20 November 1913.

Ministers and doctors may depart from the faith, as the Word declares they will, and as the messages that God has given His servant declare they will. Thus believers will be given evidence that the Word of God, the warnings He has given, are being fulfilled right among us. Some may make light of these messages, misinterpret them, and say untruthful things, which lead others' minds astray. —*7MR* 192, 193.

There will be an army of steadfast believers who will stand as firm as a rock through the last test. But where in that army are those who have been standard-bearers? Where are those whose voices have sounded in proclaiming the truth to the sinning? Some of them are not there. We look for them, but in the time of shaking they have been unable to stand, and have passed over to the enemy's ranks.—*RH* 24 December 1889.

Many will show that they are not one with Christ, that they are not dead to the world, that they may live with him; and frequent will be the apostasies of men who have occupied responsible positions.—*RH* 11 September 1888.

The days are fast approaching when there will be great perplexity and confusion. Satan, clothed with angel robes, will deceive, if possible, the very elect. There will be gods many and lords many. Every wind of doctrine will be blowing. Those who have rendered supreme homage to "science falsely so called" will not be the leaders then. Those who have trusted to intellect, genius, or talent will not then stand at the head of rank and file. They did not keep pace with the light. Those who have proved themselves unfaithful will not then be entrusted with the flock. In the last solemn work few great men will be engaged. They are self-sufficient, independent of God, and He cannot use them.—*5T* 80.

As the storm [of persecution] approaches, a large class who have professed faith in the third angel's message, but have not been sanctified through obedience to the truth, abandon their position, and join the ranks of the opposition. By uniting with the world and partaking of its spirit, they have come to view matters in nearly the same light; and when the test is brought, they are prepared to choose the easy, popular side. Men of talent and pleasing address, who once rejoiced in the truth, employ their powers to deceive and mislead souls. They become the most bitter enemies of their former brethren. When Sabbath-keepers are brought before the courts to answer for their faith, these apostates are the most efficient agents of Satan to misrepresent and accuse them, and by false reports and insinuations to stir up the rulers against them.—*GC* 608.

When the religion of Christ is most held in contempt, when His law is most despised, then should our zeal be the warmest and our courage and firmness the most unflinching. To stand in defense of truth and righteousness when the majority forsake us, to fight the battles of the Lord when champions are few—this will be our test. At this time we must gather warmth from the coldness of others, courage from their cowardice, and loyalty from their treason. The nation [the United States] will be on the side of the great rebel leader.—*5T* 136.

Separation and unity

As trials thicken around us, both separation and unity will be seen in our ranks. Some who are now ready to take up weapons of warfare will in times of real peril make it manifest that they have not built upon the solid rock; they will yield to temptation. Those who have had great light and precious privileges, but have not improved them, will, under one pretext or another, go out from us.—*6T* 400.

All who wish to draw off from the body will have opportunity. Something will arise to test everyone. The great sifting time is just before us.—*1T* 251.

Things that will cause the shaking or sifting

The Straight Testimony

I asked [the angel] the meaning of the shaking I had seen. I was shown that it would be caused by the straight testimony called forth by the counsel of the true Witness to the Laodiceans. It will have its effect upon the heart of the receiver of the testimony, and it will lead him to exalt the standard and pour forth the straight truth. This straight testimony some will not bear. They will rise up against it, and this will cause a shaking among God's people.—*1SG* 184.

One thing is certain: Those Seventh-day Adventists who take their stand under Satan's banner will first give up their faith in the warnings and reproofs contained in the Testimonies[111] of God's Spirit.—*3SM* 84.

Just as long as God has a church, he will have those who will cry aloud and spare not, who will be his instruments to reprove selfishness and sins, and will not shun to declare the whole counsel of God, whether men will hear or forbear. I saw that individuals would rise up against the plain testimonies. It does not suit their natural feelings. They would choose to have smooth things spoken unto them, and have peace cried in their ears. . . . The shaking must soon take place to purify the church.—*2SG* 284.

There will be a hatred kindled against the testimonies which is satanic. The workings of Satan will be to unsettle the faith of the churches in them, for this reason: Satan cannot have so clear a track to bring in his deceptions and bind up souls in his delusions if the warnings and reproofs and counsels of the Spirit of God are heeded.—*1SM* 48.

False Prophets
Every conceivable message is coming to counterfeit the work of God, and always bearing the inscription of truth upon its banner. And those who are prepared for anything new and sensational, will handle these things in such a manner that our enemies will charge all that is inconsistent and overdone upon Mrs. E. G. White, the prophetess. . . .

There will be counterfeit messages coming from persons in all directions. One after another [these] will rise up, appearing to be inspired, when they have not the inspiration of heaven, but are under the deception of the enemy. All who receive their messages will be led astray.—*3SM* 404.

The light given me has been . . . that many would go out from us, giving

---

111. Ellen White frequently referred to the Spirit of Prophecy writings as "the testimonies," or "the testimonies of the Spirit of God."

heed to seducing spirits and doctrines of devils. The Lord desires that every soul who claims to believe the truth shall have an intelligent knowledge of what is truth. False prophets will arise and will deceive many. Everything is to be shaken that can be shaken.—*Ev* 363.

There will be those who will claim to have visions. When God gives you clear evidence that the vision is from Him, you may accept it, but do not accept it on any other evidence; for people are going to be led more and more astray in foreign countries and in America. The Lord wants His people to act like men and women of sense.

In the future, deception of every kind is to arise, and we want solid ground for our feet. We want solid pillars for the building. Not one pin is to be removed from that which the Lord has established.—*RH* 25 May 1905.

Miracles of Healing

Works of apparent healing will bring Seventh-day Adventists to the test. Many who have had great light will fail to walk in the light, because they have not become one with Christ.[112]—*2SM* 53.

Some [Seventh-day Adventists] will be tempted to receive these wonders as from God. The sick will be healed before us. Miracles will be performed in our sight. . . . By departing from the plain precepts and commandments of God, and giving heed to fables, the minds of many are preparing to receive these lying wonders.—*1T* 302.

Heresies

The days are fast approaching when there will be great perplexity and confusion in the religious world. There will be gods many and lords many; every wind of doctrine will be blowing; and Satan, clothed in angel robes, would deceive, if it were possible, the very elect.—*W* 25 December 1906; cf *5T* 80.

Heresies will come in among . . . [God's people] which will sift them,

---

112. Even now, there are Seventh-day Adventists who are going to the "god of Ekron" (2 Kings 1:2-4) for healing—*because he offers instant relief!* Instead of going to Satan's healers, they should seek the Great Physician, and if He does not see fit to heal them, they rest in the promise that His "grace is sufficient" (2 Cor. 12:7-9).

separating the chaff from the wheat.—*5T* 707.

When the shaking comes, by the introduction of false theories, . . . surface readers, anchored nowhere, are like shifting sand. They slide into any position to suit the tenor of their feelings of bitterness.—*TM* 112.

In the future, deception of every kind is to arise, and we want solid ground for our feet. . . . The enemy will bring in false theories, such as the doctrine that there is no sanctuary.[113] This is one of the points on which there will be a departing from the faith.—*RH* 25 May 1905.

False Shepherds Will Proclaim False Messages

Many will stand in our pulpits with the torch of false prophecy in their hands, kindled from the hellish torch of Satan. . . .

Some will go out from among us who will bear the ark[114] no longer. —*TM* 409-411.

There will be, even among us, hirelings and wolves in sheep's clothing who will [try to] persuade the flock of God to sacrifice unto other gods[115] before the Lord. . . . Youth who are not established, rooted and grounded in the truth, will be corrupted and drawn away by the blind leaders of the blind.—*3SM* 398.

Before the great [time of] trouble shall come upon the world such as has never been since there was a nation, those who have faltered and who would ignorantly lead in unsafe paths will reveal this before the real vital test, the last proving, comes, so that whatsoever they may say will not be regarded [by God's faithful people] as voicing the True Shepherd.—*EGW1888* 1002.

Hypnotism

The time has come when even in the church and in our institutions, some will depart from the faith, giving heed to seducing spirits and doctrines of

---

113. Even now there are professed Seventh-day Adventists who in one way or another question our doctrine of the sanctuary.

114. This is speaking particularly concerning Seventh-day Adventist ministers; for it is they who stand in our pulpits and, figuratively speaking, bear the ark of God.

115. "Sunday" is often called "the idol sabbath" by Ellen White (e.g., *EGW1888* 477; cf *RH* 16 April 1890). This statement seems to indicate that some Seventh-day Adventist pastors will try to persuade their flocks to worship the papal "idol."

devils. . . . Let us bear a plain, clear testimony right to the point, that hypnotism is being used by those who have departed from the faith,[116] and that we are not to link up with them. Through those who depart from the faith, the power of the enemy will be exercised to lead others astray.—*3SM* 411, 412; *Lt* 237, 1904.

The sciences of phrenology,[117] psychology, and mesmerism are the channel through which . . . [Satan] comes more directly to this generation and works with that power which is to characterize his efforts near the close of probation.—*1T* 290.

At the Great Heart of the Work
At the great heart of the work, Satan will use his hellish arts to the utmost. He will seek in every possible way to interpose himself between the people and God, and shut away the light that God would have come to his children. It is his design to keep them in ignorance of what shall come upon the earth.—*RH* 24 December 1889.

Apostasy and how to counteract it
Rebellion and apostasy are in the very air we breathe. We shall be affected by them unless we by faith hang our helpless souls upon Christ. If men are so easily misled now, how will they stand when Satan shall personate Christ, and work miracles? Who will be unmoved by his misrepresentations then—professing to be Christ when it is only Satan assuming the person of Christ, and apparently working the works of Christ?—*2SM* 394; *Lt* 203, 1905.

Only those who have been diligent students of the Scriptures, and who have received the love of the truth, will be shielded from the powerful

---

116. There are Seventh-day Adventists who advocate the use of hypnotism in the treatment of certain psychosomatic illnesses.

117. Phrenology was a pseudoscience that was popular during the mid-nineteenth century. Practitioners of this "science" claimed to be able to discern character and personality by examining the shape of a person's head. Psychology, as used in the mid-nineteenth century, was frequently meant hypnotism. Mesmerism is another word for hypnotism. Apparently these pseudosciences will reemerge near the close of probation as an important aspect of Satan's efforts to deceive.

delusion [Satan's personation of Christ] that takes the world captive. By the Bible testimony these will detect the deceiver in his disguise. To all, the testing time will come. By the sifting of temptation, the genuine Christian will be revealed. Are the people of God now so firmly established upon His word that they would not yield to the evidence of their senses?—*GC* 625.

The alpha and omega of apostasy

Before the last developments of the work of apostasy there will be a confusion of faith. There will not be clear and definite ideas concerning the mystery of God. One truth after another will be corrupted.—*ST* 28 May 1894.

Be not deceived; many will depart from the faith, giving heed to seducing spirits and doctrines of devils. We have now before us [in Dr. John Harvey Kellogg's pantheistic teachings] the alpha of this danger. The omega will be of a most startling nature.—*7MR* 188; *Lt* 263, 1904.

There is in . . . [pantheism] the beginning of theories which, carried to their logical conclusion, would destroy faith in the sanctuary question and in the atonement.—*2MR* 243.

We are now to be on guard, and not drawn away from the all-important message given of God for this time. Satan is not ignorant of the result of trying to define God and Jesus Christ in a spiritualistic way that sets God and Christ as a nonentity. The moments occupied in this kind of science are, in the place of preparing the way of the Lord, making a way for Satan to come in and confuse the minds with mysticisms of his own devising. Although they are dressed up in angel robes they have made our God and our Christ a nonentity. Why?—because Satan sees the minds are all fitted for his working. Men have lost track of Christ and the Lord God, and have been obtaining an experience that is Omega to one of the most subtle delusions that will ever captivate the minds of men. We are forbidden to . . . set the imagination in a train of conjecture.—*11MR* 211.

If God has ever spoken by me, you will before long hear of a wonderful science—a science of the devil. Its aim will be to make of no account God and Jesus Christ whom He has sent. Some will exalt this false science, and through them Satan will seek to make void the law of God. Great miracles will be performed in the sight of men in behalf of this wonderful science.—*3SM* 408; *Lt* 48, 1907.

The decrease/increase paradox

When the religion of Christ is most held in contempt, when His law is most despised, then should our zeal be the warmest and our courage and firmness the most unflinching. To stand in defense of truth and righteousness when the majority forsake us, to fight the battles of the Lord when champions are few—this will be our test.—*5T* 136.

The church may appear as about to fall, but it does not fall. It remains, while the sinners in Zion will be sifted out—the chaff separated from the precious wheat.[118] This is a terrible ordeal, but nevertheless it must take place.—*7BC* 911.

I saw our people in great distress, weeping and praying, pleading the sure promises of God, while the wicked were all around us, mocking us and threatening to destroy us. They ridiculed our feebleness, they mocked at the smallness of our numbers.—*2MR* 207.

Satan, in cooperation with his angels and with evil men, will put forth every effort to gain the victory, and will appear to succeed.[119] But from this conflict, truth and righteousness will come forth triumphant in victory.—*10MR* 338.

The Lord will work so that the disaffected ones will be separated from the true and loyal ones. Those who, like Cornelius, will fear God and

---

118. In the past, when God's people have backslidden into apostasy, He has raised up a new organization, but this is not what He does with His remnant people. Rather than raising up a new organization, the sinners in Zion are sifted out. In other words, Seventh-day Adventism (not necessarily the Seventh-day Adventist organization as it is known today) will survive, but obviously in not exactly the same form as it now exists.

119. From the human viewpoint Satan appears to succeed—he succeeds in drawing off from the church visible those who have compromised with the world. But as members of the church invisible, who are still in spiritual Babylon, heed the call to forsake her under the latter rain, their numbers will swell the ranks of the remnant church and the third angel's message triumphs gloriously.

glorify Him, will take their places. The ranks will not be diminished.[120] Those who are firm and true will close up the vacancies that are made by those who become offended and apostatize.—*2MR* 57.

The broken ranks will be filled up by those represented by Christ as coming in at the eleventh hour. There are many with whom the Spirit of God is striving. The time of God's destructive judgments is the time of mercy for those who [until then] have [had] no opportunity to learn what is truth. Tenderly will the Lord look upon them. His heart of mercy is touched. His hand is still stretched out to save, while the door is closed to those who would not enter. Large numbers will be admitted [into the church visible] who in these last days hear the truth for the first time.—*LDE* 182; cf *9T* 97.

The probation of those who know the truth closes first

I speak not my own words when I say that God's Spirit will pass by those who have had their day of test and opportunity, but who have not distinguished the voice of God or appreciated the movings of His Spirit. Then thousands in the eleventh hour will see and acknowledge the truth. . . . These conversions to truth will be made with a rapidity that will surprise the church [visible], and God's name alone will be glorified.[121]—*2SM* 16.

As we near the end we either advance or retrograde more rapidly

As we near the close of this earth's history, we advance more and more rapidly in Christian growth, or we retrograde just as decidedly.—*3SM* 407.

---

120. These statements are not mutually contradictory. The church visible, which we believe is the Seventh-day Adventist Church organization, includes both "sheep and goats" (Matt. 25:31-44), and in the final crisis the goats are separated from the sheep. The invisible church includes "sheep" in "other folds" (John 10:16). These will come into the church visible during the latter rain.

121. This statement clearly teaches that the probation of those who have known the third angel's message, but have not been sanctified by the truth, closes before the probation of those who have never before had an opportunity to know the message.

THE LOUD CRY, THE ANGEL OF REVELATION 18, AND THE LATTER RAIN

Latter-day messages and the latter rain

I saw another angel flying in the midst of heaven, having the everlasting gospel to preach to those who dwell on the earth—to every nation, tribe, tongue, and people—saying with a loud voice, "Fear God and give glory to Him, for the hour of His judgment has come; and worship Him who made heaven and earth, the sea and springs of water."

And another angel followed, saying, "Babylon is fallen, is fallen, that great city, because she has made all nations drink of the wine of the wrath of her fornication."

Then a third angel followed them, saying with a loud voice, "If anyone worships the beast and his image, and receives his mark on his forehead or on his hand, he himself shall also drink of the wine of the wrath of God, which is poured out full strength into the cup of His indignation."—Rev. 14:6-10, NKJV.

After these things I saw another angel coming down from heaven, having great authority, and the earth was illuminated with his glory.

And he cried mightily with a loud voice, saying, "Babylon the great is fallen, is fallen, and has become a habitation of demons, a prison for every foul spirit, and a cage for every unclean and hated bird! For all the nations have drunk of the wine of the wrath of her fornication, the kings of the earth have committed fornication with her, and the merchants of the earth have become rich through the abundance of her luxury." And I heard another voice from heaven saying, "Come out of her, my people, lest you share in her sins, and lest you receive of her plagues."—Rev. 18:1-4, NKJV.

This is what was spoken by the prophet Joel [Joel 2:28, 29]:
"And it shall come to pass in the last days, says God, that I will pour out of My Spirit on all flesh; your sons and your daughters shall prophesy, your young men shall see visions, your old men shall dream dreams. And on My menservants and on My maidservants I will pour out My Spirit in those days."—Acts 2:16-18, NKJV.

The eschatological fulfillment of these prophecies

The truth for this time, the third angel's message, is to be proclaimed with a loud voice, meaning with increasing power, as we approach the great final test. . . . The present truth for this time comprises the messages, the third angel's message succeeding the first and the second. . . . We stand as the remnant people in these last days to promulgate the truth and swell the cry of the third angel's wonderful distinct message, giving the trumpet a certain sound. Eternal truth, which we have adhered to from the beginning, is to be maintained in all its increasing importance to the close of probation.—*9MR* 291; *Ms* 67, 1909.

God has given the messages of Revelation 14 their place in the line of prophecy, and their work is not to cease till the close of this earth's history. The first and second angel's messages are still truth for this time, and are to run parallel with this which follows. The third angel proclaims his warning with a loud voice.[122] "After these things," said John, "I saw another angel

---

122. The "loud voice" of the third angel is the loud cry. (See *ISG* 193, 194, on p. 146.)

come down from heaven, having great power, and the earth was lightened with his glory." In this illumination, the light of all the three messages is combined.—*EGW1888* 804.

The third angel's message . . . is the last offer of mercy to the world, the most solemn message ever given to mortals.—*ST* 25 January 1910.

There must be no concealing of the principles of our faith. The third angel's message is to be sounded by God's people. It is to swell to the loud cry.—*PM* 389.

God still has a people in [spiritual] Babylon; and before the visitation of His judgments these faithful ones must be called out, that they "partake not of her sins and receive not of her plagues." Hence the movement symbolized by the angel [of Revelation 18] coming down from heaven, lightening the earth with his glory and crying mightily with a strong voice, announcing the sins of Babylon. In connection with his message the call is heard: "Come out of her, My people." These announcements, uniting with the third angel's message, constitute the final warning to be given to the inhabitants of the earth.—*GC* 604.

God has children, many of them, in the Protestant churches, and a large number in the Catholic churches, who are more true to obey the light and to do [to] the very best of their knowledge than a large number among Sabbathkeeping Adventists who do not walk in the light. The Lord will have the message of truth proclaimed, that Protestants may be warned and awakened to the true state of things, and consider the worth of the privilege of religious freedom which they have long enjoyed. . . .

There are many souls to come out of the ranks of the world, out of the churches—even the Catholic Church—whose zeal will far exceed that of those who have stood in the rank and file to proclaim the truth heretofore. For this reason the eleventh hour laborers will receive their penny. These will see the battle coming and will give the trumpet a certain sound. When the crisis is upon us, when the season of calamity shall come, they will come to the front, gird themselves with the whole armor of God, and exalt His law, adhere to the faith of Jesus, and maintain the cause of religious liberty which reformers defended with toil and for which they sacrificed their lives.—*3SM* 386, 387.

From quarters where we least expect will come voices urging us forward in the work of giving to the world the last message of mercy.—*20MR* 125.

The latter rain and the angel of Revelation 18

In immediate connection with the scenes of the great day of God, the Lord by the prophet Joel has promised a special manifestation of His Spirit. Joel 2:28. This prophecy received a partial fulfillment in the outpouring of the Spirit on the day of Pentecost; but it will reach its full accomplishment in the manifestation of divine grace which will attend the closing work of the gospel.—*GC* ix.

[God] will so bestow His Spirit upon His people that they will become a light amid the moral darkness; and great light will be reflected in all parts of the world.—*4BC* 1175.

While the work of salvation is closing, trouble will be coming on the earth, and the nations will be angry, yet held in check so as not to prevent the work of the third angel. At that time the "latter rain," or refreshing from the presence of the Lord, will come to give power to the loud voice of the third angel.—*EW* 85, 86.

I saw another mighty angel commissioned to descend to earth, and unite his voice with the third angel, and give power and force to his message.... The work of this angel comes in at the right time, and joins in the last great work of the third angel's message, as it swells into a loud cry.[123]—*1SG* 193, 194.

[The] message [of the angel of Rev. 18] seemed to be an addition to the third message, joining it.—*EW* 277.

---

123. The angel of Rev. 18 "gives power and force" to the third angel's message as it "swells into a loud cry."

I have no specific time of which to speak when the outpouring of the Holy Spirit will take place,—when the mighty angel [of Rev. 18] will come down from heaven, and unite with the third angel[124] in closing up the work for this world.—*RH* 29 March 1892.

Those who follow in the light need have no anxiety lest that in the outpouring of the latter rain they will not be baptized with the Holy Spirit.[125] If we would receive the light of the glorious angel [of Rev. 18] that shall lighten the earth with his glory, let us see to it that our hearts are cleansed, emptied of self, and turned toward heaven, that they may be ready for the latter rain.—*ST* 1 August 1892.

In the last work God will work in unexpected ways

I stated that . . . another angel was to come from heaven with a message, and the whole earth was to be lightened with his glory. It would be impossible for us to state just how this additional light would come. It might come in a very unexpected manner, in a way that would not agree with the ideas that many have conceived.—*13MR* 334; *Lt* 22, 1889.

Unless those who can help are roused to a sense of their duty, they will not recognize the work of God when the loud cry of the third angel shall be heard. When light goes forth to lighten the earth, instead of coming up to the help of the Lord, they will want to bind about His work to meet their narrow ideas. . . . [T]he Lord will work in this last work in a manner very much out of the common order of things, and in a way that will be contrary to any human planning.—*2MR* 19.

If God's people make no efforts on their part, but wait for the refreshing [i.e., latter rain] to come upon them and remove their wrongs and correct their errors; if they depend upon that to cleanse them from filthiness of the

---

124. The descent of the angel of Rev. 18 is frequently equated with the outpouring of the latter rain (e.g., *RH* 21 April 1891; *ST* 1 August 1892; *RH* 21 July 1896).
125. Some seem to think that God will pour out the latter rain on the church in its present condition. This is a mistake that could lead to being deceived by Satan's false latter rain, which *precedes* the true latter rain (*GC* 464). The true latter rain is not poured out until *after* the shaking. This is why *Spiritual Gifts,* 2:284, says that "the shaking must soon take place to purify the church."

flesh and spirit, and fit them to engage in the loud cry of the third angel, they will be found wanting. The refreshing or power of God comes only on those who have prepared themselves for it by doing the work which God bids them, namely, cleansing themselves from all filthiness of the flesh and spirit, perfecting holiness in the fear of God.—*1T* 619.

The third angel's message is to lighten the earth with its glory; but only those who have withstood temptation in the strength of the Mighty One will be permitted to act a part in proclaiming it when it shall have swelled into the loud cry.—*HS* 155.

There is to be in the [Seventh-day Adventist] churches a wonderful manifestation of the power of God, but it will not move upon those who have not humbled themselves before the Lord, and opened the door of the heart by confession and repentance. In the manifestation of that power which lightens the earth with the glory of God, they will see only something which in their blindness they think dangerous, something which will arouse their fears, and they will brace themselves to resist it. Because the Lord does not work according to their ideas and expectations, they will oppose the work. "Why," they [will] say, "should not we know the Spirit of God, when we have been in the work so many years?"—*RH* Extra 23 December 1890.

Warning: the false latter rain precedes the true latter rain

God has honest children among the nominal Adventists and the fallen churches, and before the plagues shall be poured out, ministers and people will be called out from these churches and will gladly receive the truth. Satan knows this; and before the loud cry of the third angel is given, he raises an excitement in these religious bodies that those who have rejected the truth may think that God is with them. He hopes to deceive the honest and lead them to think that God is still working for the churches.—*EW* 261.

Before the final visitation of God's judgments upon the earth, there will be, among the people of the Lord, such a revival of primitive godliness as has not been witnessed since apostolic times. The Spirit and power of God will be poured out upon His children. At that time many will separate themselves from those churches in which the love of this world has supplanted love for God and His word. Many, both of ministers and people, will gladly accept those great truths which God has caused to be proclaimed at this time, to prepare a people for the Lord's second coming. The enemy of souls desires to hinder this work; and before the time for such a movement shall come, he will endeavor to prevent it, by introducing a counterfeit. In those churches which he can bring under his deceptive power, he will make it appear that God's special blessing is poured out; there will be manifest what is thought to be great religious interest. Multitudes will exult that God is working marvelously for them, when the work is that of another spirit. Under a religious guise, Satan will seek to extend his influence over the Christian world.—*GC* 464.

Through spiritualism, Satan appears as a benefactor of the race, healing the diseases of the people, and professing to present a new and more exalted system of religious faith.—*GC* 589.

There is a wonder-working power to appear: and it will be when men are claiming sanctification, and holiness, lifting themselves up higher and higher and boasting of themselves.—*3SM* 353.

The devil has device after device, and he carries them out in ways that . . . [Seventh-day Adventists] do not expect. Satan's agencies will invent ways to make sinners out of saints.

I tell you now, that when I am laid to rest, great changes will take place. I do not know when I shall be taken; and I desire to warn all against the devices of the devil. I want people to know that I warned them fully before my death. I do not know especially what changes will take place; but they should watch every conceivable sin that Satan will try to immortalize.[126]—*Ms* 1, 1915.

Some look with horror upon one deception, while they readily receive another. Satan deceives some with Spiritualism. He also comes as an angel of light and spreads his influence over the land by means of false

---

126. See *Selected Messages*, 3:353, quoted above.

reformations. The churches are elated, and consider that God is working marvelously for them, when it is the work of another spirit.[127]—*EW* 261.

Manifestations of the false latter rain

The things you have described as taking place in [Cicero] Indiana, the Lord has shown me would take place just before the close of probation. Every uncouth thing will be demonstrated. There will be shouting, with drums, music, and dancing.[128] The senses of rational beings will become so confused that they cannot be trusted to make right decisions. And this is called the moving of the Holy Spirit.

The Holy Spirit never reveals itself in such methods, in such a bedlam of noise. This is an invention of Satan to cover up his ingenious methods for making of none effect the pure, sincere, elevating, ennobling, sanctifying truth for this time.—*2SM* 36.

In the last days the enemy of present truth will bring in manifestations that are not in harmony with the workings of the Spirit, but are calculated to lead astray those who stand ready to take up with something new and strange.—*2SM* 41.

Some important events leading up to the true latter rain

"The commencement of that time of trouble," . . . mentioned [in *EW* 33] does not refer to the time when the plagues shall begin to be poured out, but to a short period just before they are poured out, while Christ is in the sanctuary. At that time, while the work of salvation is closing, trouble will be coming on the earth, and the nations will be angry, yet held in check so as not to prevent the work of the third angel. At that time the "latter rain," or refreshing from the presence of the Lord, will come, to give power to the loud voice of the third angel, and prepare the saints to stand in the period when the seven last plagues shall be poured out.—*EW* 85, 86.

---

127. The true latter rain is not poured out until God's people are purified by the shaking. "Before giving the baptism of the Holy Spirit, our heavenly Father will try us, to see if we can live without dishonoring Him" (*3SM* 426, 427).

128. If Seventh-day Adventist churches follow the charismatic road, down which some Christian denominations are traveling, will our churches recognize these manifestations of the false latter rain?

Laws enforcing the observance of Sunday as the Sabbath will bring about a national apostasy from the principles of republicanism upon which the government [of the United States] has been founded. The religion of the papacy will be accepted by the rulers, and the law of God will be made void.

When the fifth seal was opened, John the Revelator saw beneath the altar the company that were slain for the word of God and the testimony of Jesus Christ. After this[129] came the scenes described in the eighteenth of Revelation,[130] when those who are faithful and true are called out from Babylon.—*20MR* 14.

Satan's agents have not been sparing of the blood of the saints. Christ's true followers are kind, tender, pitiful. They will realize the meaning of the work of the angel of Revelation eighteen, who is to lighten the whole earth with his glory while he cries with a loud voice, "Babylon the great is fallen, is fallen" (Rev. 18:2). Many will heed this call.

We need to study the pouring out of the seventh vial. The powers of evil will not yield up the conflict without a struggle. But providence has a part to act in the battle of Armageddon. When the earth is lighted with the glory of the angel of Revelation 18, the religious elements, good and evil, will awake from slumber, and the armies of the living God will take the field.—*Ms* 175, 1899; not all quoted in *7BC* 983.

A detailed sequence of events leading up to the latter rain

In the last work for the warning of the world, two distinct calls are made to the churches. The second angel's message is, "Babylon is fallen, is fallen, that great city, because she made all nations drink of the wine of the wrath of her fornication" (Rev. 14:8). And in the loud cry of the third angel's message a voice is heard from heaven saying, "Come out of her, my people, that ye be not partakers of her sins, and that ye receive not of her plagues. For her sins have reached unto heaven, and God hath remembered her iniquities."—*RH* 6 December 1892.

---

129. Notice that it is not until America makes void God's law and the death penalty is enforced against Sabbath keepers that the angel of Revelation 18 calls God's people out of spiritual Babylon (cf *GC* 605-612).

130. The call of Revelation 18 for God's people to leave spiritual Babylon is given *after* many of God's people are martyred.

Heretofore those who presented the truths of the third angel's message have often been regarded as mere alarmists. Their predictions that religious intolerance would gain control in the United States, that church and state would unite to persecute those who keep the commandments of God, have been pronounced groundless and absurd. . . . But as the question of enforcing Sunday observance is widely agitated, the event so long doubted and disbelieved is seen to be approaching, and the third message will produce an effect which it could not have had before. . . .

As the time comes for . . . [the third angel's message] to be given with greatest power, the Lord will work through humble instruments, leading the minds of those who consecrate themselves to His service. . . . Men of faith and prayer will be constrained to go forth with holy zeal, declaring the words which God gives them. The sins of Babylon will be laid open. [In the populous cities of the land, and in the places where men have gone to the greatest lengths in speaking against the Most High, the voice of stern rebuke will be heard. Boldly will men of God's appointment denounce the union of the church with the world.[131]]. The fearful results of enforcing the observances of the church by civil authority, the inroads of Spiritualism, the stealthy but rapid progress of the papal power,—all will be unmasked. By these solemn warnings the people will be stirred. Thousands upon thousands will listen who have never heard words like these. In amazement they hear the testimony that Babylon is the church, fallen because of her errors and sins, because of her rejection of the truth sent to her from heaven. As the people go to their former teachers with the eager inquiry, Are these things so? the ministers present fables, prophesy smooth things, to soothe their fears, and quiet the awakened conscience. But since many refuse to be satisfied with the mere authority of men, and demand a plain "Thus saith the Lord," the popular ministry, . . . filled with anger as their authority is questioned, will denounce the message as of Satan, and stir up the sin-loving multitudes to revile and persecute those who proclaim it.

As the controversy extends into new fields, and the minds of the people are called to God's down-trodden law, Satan is astir. The power attending the message will only madden those who oppose it. The clergy will put forth almost superhuman efforts to shut away the light, lest it should shine

---

131. *PK* 187.

upon their flocks. By every means at their command they will endeavor to suppress the discussion of these vital questions. The church appeals to the strong arm of civil power, and in this work, papists and Protestants[132] unite.

As the movement for Sunday enforcement becomes more bold and decided, the law will be invoked[133] against commandment-keepers. They will be threatened with fines and imprisonment, and some will be offered positions of influence, and other rewards and advantages, as inducements to renounce their faith. . . . Those who are arraigned before the courts, make a strong vindication of the truth, and some who hear them are led to take their stand to keep all the commandments of God. Thus light will be brought before thousands who otherwise would know nothing of these truths.

Conscientious obedience to the word of God will be treated as rebellion. Blinded by Satan, the parent will exercise harshness and severity toward the believing child; the master or mistress will oppress the commandment-keeping servant. Affection will be alienated; children will be disinherited, and driven from home. . . . As the defenders of truth refuse to honor the Sunday-sabbath, some of them will be thrust into prison, some will be exiled, some will be treated as slaves. . . .

As the storm approaches, a large class who have professed faith in the third angel's message, but have not been sanctified through obedience to the truth, abandon their position, and join the ranks of the opposition. By uniting with the world and partaking of its spirit, they have come to view matters in nearly the same light; and when the test is brought, they are prepared to choose the easy, popular side. Men of talent and pleasing address, who once rejoiced in the truth, employ their powers to deceive and mislead souls. They become the most bitter enemies of their former brethren. When Sabbath-keepers are brought before the courts to answer for their faith, these apostates are the most efficient agents of Satan to misrepresent and accuse them, and by false reports and insinuations to stir up the rulers against them.

---

132. *Testimonies for the Church,* 5:712, says: "When our nation [the United States of America] shall so abjure the principles of its government as to enact a Sunday law, Protestantism will in this act join hands with popery." This statement helps relate events in this section of *The Great Controversy* to other cause-effect events found elsewhere in the Spirit of Prophecy writings.
133. *Manuscript Releases,* 5:78, says that "when" "divine honors" are "fully" placed "upon a false sabbath," "persecution will break forth upon those who observe the Sabbath that God gave."

[In the great closing work we shall meet with perplexities that we know not how to deal with; but let us not forget that the three great powers of heaven are working, that a divine hand is on the wheel, and that God will bring His promises to pass.[134]] In this time of persecution the faith of the Lord's servants will be tried. They have faithfully given the warning, looking to God and to His word alone. God's Spirit, moving upon their hearts, has constrained them to speak. Stimulated with holy zeal, and with the divine impulse strong upon them, they entered upon the performance of their duties without coldly calculating the consequences of speaking to the people the word which the Lord had given them. They have not consulted their temporal interests, nor sought to preserve their reputation or their lives. Yet when the storm of opposition and reproach bursts upon them, some, overwhelmed with consternation, will be ready to exclaim, "Had we foreseen the consequences of our words, we would have held our peace." They are hedged in with difficulties. Satan assails them with fierce temptations. The work which they have undertaken seems far beyond their ability to accomplish. They are threatened with destruction. The enthusiasm which animated them is gone; yet they cannot turn back. Then, feeling their utter helplessness, they flee to the Mighty One for strength. . . . [The Lord will interpose when . . . none but a divine power can counteract the satanic agencies at work. When His people shall be in the greatest danger, seemingly unable to stand against the power of Satan, God will work in their behalf.[135]]

As the opposition rises to a fiercer height,[136] the servants of God are again perplexed; for it seems to them that they have brought [on] the crisis. But conscience and the word of God assure them that their course is right; and although the trials continue, they are strengthened to bear them. The contest grows closer and sharper, but their faith and courage rise with the emergency. . . .

The angel who unites in the proclamation of the third angel's message, is to lighten the whole earth with his glory. [The work of this angel comes in at the right time, and joins in the last great work of the third angel's

---

134. *8T* 254.

135. *2SM* 373.

136. "When the storm of persecution really breaks upon us, the true sheep will hear the true Shepherd's voice. Self-denying efforts will be put forth to save the lost, and many who have strayed from the fold will come back to follow the great Shepherd" (*6T* 401).

message as it swells into a loud cry.[137]] [When divine power is combined with human effort, the work will spread like fire in the stubble.[138]] [Angels . . . {will be} sent to aid the mighty angel from heaven, and . . . voices {will be heard} which . . . {seem} to sound everywhere, "Come out of her {mystical Babylon}, My people, that ye be not partakers of her sins, and that ye receive not of her plagues."[139]] [Those who could not by reasoning overcome Satanic delusions, will bear an affirmative testimony that will baffle supposedly learned men. Words will come from the lips of the unlearned with such convincing power and wisdom that conversions will be made to the truth. Thousands will be converted under their testimony.[140]] A work of world-wide extent and unwonted power is here foretold. . . . The work will be similar to that of the day of Pentecost. As the "former rain" was given, in the outpouring of the Holy Spirit at the opening of the gospel, to cause the upspringing of the precious seed, so the "latter rain" will be given at its close, for the ripening of the harvest. [God will employ agencies whose origin man will be unable to discern; angels will do a work which men might have had the blessing of accomplishing,[141] had they not neglected to answer the claims of God.[142]]—*GC* 605-611.

We have taught, we have expected, that an angel is to come down from heaven, that the earth will be lightened with his glory. Then we shall behold an ingathering of souls similar to that witnessed on the day of pentecost.—*GCDB* 1 February 1893.

As the members of Christ's body approach the period of their final conflict they will grow up into him, and will possess symmetrical

---

137. *1SG* 194. This angel's message is not the loud cry; rather the power with which he descends from heaven increases the loud cry of the third angel's message. This is why *Early Writings*, 277, says that the message of the angel of Revelation 18 "seemed to be an addition to the third [angel's] message."
138. *RH* 15 December 1885.
139. *EW* 277.
140. *8MR* 187.
141. Human nature being what it is, there is little hope that any generation, past, present, or future will ever "finish the work." Yet God's work will be finished—angels will aid in accomplishment of the task. But notice that this only happens *after* the shaking and only involves those who work faithfully and in cooperation with God.
142. *RH* 15 December 1885.

characters. As the message of the third angel swells to a loud cry, great power and glory will attend the closing work. It is the latter rain, which revives and strengthens the people of God to pass through the time of Jacob's trouble referred to by the prophets. The glory of that light which attends the third angel will be reflected upon them. God will preserve his people through that time of peril.—*ST* 27 November 1879.

The great work of the gospel is not to close with less manifestation of the power of God than marked its opening. . . . Here are "the times of refreshing" to which the apostle Peter looked forward when he said, "Repent ye therefore, and be converted, that your sins may be blotted out when the times of refreshing shall come from the presence of the Lord; and He shall send Jesus."

Servants of God, with their faces lighted up and shining with holy consecration, will hasten from place to place to proclaim the message from heaven. By thousands of voices, all over the earth, the warning will be given. Miracles will be wrought, the sick will be healed, and signs and wonders will follow the believers. Satan also works with lying wonders, even bringing down fire from heaven in the sight of men. Thus the inhabitants of the earth will be brought to take their stand. [Minds will be fully prepared to make decisions for or against the truth.[143]]

The message will be carried not so much by argument as by the deep conviction of the Spirit of God. The arguments have been presented. The seed has been sown, and now it will spring up and bear fruit. The publications distributed by missionary workers have exerted their influence, yet many whose minds were impressed have been prevented from fully comprehending the truth or from yielding obedience. Now the rays of light penetrate everywhere, the truth is seen in its clearness, and the honest children of God sever the bands which have held them. Family connections, church relations, are powerless to stay them now. Truth is more precious than all besides.—*GC* 611, 612.

Those who had been bound; some wives who had been bound by their husbands, and some children had been bound by their parents . . . , now

---

143. *1SAT* 87.

eagerly laid hold of . . . [the message]. All fear of their relatives was gone. The truth alone was exalted to them. It was dearer and more precious than life.—*1T* 182, 183.

Clad in the armor of Christ's righteousness, the church is to enter upon her final conflict. "Fair as the moon, clear as the sun, and terrible as an army with banners" (Cant. 6:10), she is to go forth into all the world, conquering and to conquer.—*RH* 1 July 1915.

The triumph of the loud cry of the third angel's message

Through most wonderful workings of divine providence, mountains of difficulty will be removed. The message that means so much to the dwellers upon earth will be heard and understood. Men will know what is truth. Onward and still onward, the work will advance, until the whole earth shall have been warned. And then shall the end come.—*RH* 22 November 1906.

I was pointed down to the time when the third angel's message was closing. The power of God had rested upon his people. They had accomplished their work, and were prepared for the trying hour before them. They had received the latter rain, or refreshing from the presence of the Lord, and the living testimony had been revived. The last great warning had sounded every where, and it had stirred up and enraged the inhabitants of earth, who would not receive the message.—*1SG* 197.

Men and women . . . so filled will they be by the Spirit of God that they will pass from country to country, from city to city, proclaiming the message of truth.—*UL* 16.

Many . . . will be seen hurrying hither and thither, constrained by the Spirit of God to bring the light to others. The truth, the Word of God, is as a fire in their bones, filling them with a burning desire to enlighten those who sit in darkness. Many, even among the uneducated, now proclaim the words of the Lord. Children are impelled by the Spirit to go forth and declare the message from heaven. The Spirit is poured out upon all who will yield to its promptings, and casting off all man's machinery, his binding rules and cautious methods, they will declare the truth with the might of the Spirit's power. Multitudes will receive the faith and join the armies of the Lord.—*RH* 23 July 1895.

Those who have held the beginning of their confidence firm unto the end will be wide-awake during the time that the third angel's message is proclaimed with great power. During the loud cry, the church, aided by the providential interpositions of her exalted Lord, will diffuse the knowledge of salvation so abundantly that light will be communicated to every city and town. The earth will be filled with the knowledge of salvation. So abundantly will the renewing Spirit of God have crowned with success the intensely active agencies, that the light of present truth will be see flashing everywhere.—*RH* 13 October 1904.

Notwithstanding the agencies combined against the truth, a large number take their stand upon the Lord's side.—*GC* 612.

Nine
C H A P T E R

THE CLOSE OF PROBATION, THE PLAGUES, AND THE DEATH DECREE

Events that happen when probation closes, from the Bible

When that time comes, all doing wrong will do it more and more; the vile will become more vile; good men will be better; those who are holy will continue on in greater holiness. See, I am coming soon, and my reward is with me, to repay everyone according to the deeds he has done.[144]— Rev. 22:, 11, 12, TLB.

At that time Michael, the great prince, the protector of your people, shall arise. There shall be a time of anguish, such as has never occurred since nations first came into existence—Dan. 12:1, NRSV.

---

144. An individual's probation closes when he dies. It also closes when, like Judas, he commits the unpardonable sin (see *DA* 654, 655). It closes for humanity when the last person makes his decision, either for God or for Satan, at which time Christ ceases his mediation in the heavenly sanctuary. When Ellen White speaks of the close of probation, she is usually referring to the close of human probation. This chapter focuses on the close of probation of humanity, although it will also deal with those who have made their decision concerning the third angel's message *before* the image-to-the-beast test.

I saw another sign in heaven, . . . seven angels having the seven last plagues, for in them the wrath of God is complete. . . . After these things I looked, and behold, the temple of the tabernacle of the testimony in heaven was opened. And out of the temple came the seven angels having the seven plagues. . . . The temple was filled with smoke from the glory of God and from His power, and no one was able to enter the temple till the seven plagues of the seven angels were completed.

Then I heard a loud voice from the temple saying to the seven angels, "Go and pour out the bowls of the wrath of God on the earth."—Rev. 15:1, 5, 6, 8; 16:1, NKJV.

The death decree of the beast of Revelation 13:11

Then I saw another beast coming up out of the earth, and he had two horns like a lamb and spoke like a dragon. . . . He was granted power to give breath to the image of the beast, that the image of the beast should both speak and cause as many as would not worship the image of the beast to be killed—Rev. 13:11, 15, NKJV.

The righteous will be saved out of the time of Jacob's trouble

Alas! For that day is great, so that none is like it; and it is the time of Jacob's trouble, but he shall be saved out of it.—Jer. 30:7, NKJV.

God's people are assured of bread and water

He will dwell on high; his place of defense will be the fortress of rocks; bread will be given him, his water will be sure.—Isa. 33:16, NKJV.

The extent of information available

Many entertain the view that probation is granted after Jesus leaves His work as mediator in the most holy apartment. This is the sophistry of Satan. God tests and proves the world by the light which He is pleased to give them previous to the coming of Christ. Characters are then formed for life or death. But the probation of those who choose to live a life of sin, and neglect the great salvation offered, closes when Christ's ministration ceases just previous to His appearing in the clouds of heaven.—*2T* 691.

The Lord has no future probation for any soul that lives. Those who do not appreciate this present probation will have no second trial. Those who in this life pursue a course which will close against them the gates of the city of God, need not flatter themselves that the Lord will give them another opportunity to prepare to meet Him.—*21MR* 398.

The events connected with the close of probation and the work of preparation for the time of trouble, are clearly presented. But multitudes have no more understanding of these important truths than if they had never been revealed. Satan watches to catch away every impression that would make them wise unto salvation, and the time of trouble will find them unready.—*GC* 594.

When the work of investigation shall be ended, when the cases of those who in all ages have professed to be followers of Christ have been examined and decided, then, and not till then, probation will close, and the door of mercy will be shut.—*GC* 428.

Probation is ended a short time before the appearing of the Lord in the clouds of heaven.—*GC* 490.

When our High Priest has finished his work in the Sanctuary, he will stand up, put on the garments of vengeance, and then the seven last plagues will be poured out. I saw that the four angels would hold the four winds until Jesus' work was done in the Sanctuary, and then will come the seven last plagues. These plagues enraged the wicked against the righteous, and they thought that we had brought them down upon them, and if they could rid the earth of us, then the plagues would be stayed. A decree went forth to slay the saints, which caused them to cry day and night for deliverance. This was the time of Jacob's trouble.—*PT* 1 August 1849.

The door of mercy closed for some but open for others

Oh that the [professed] people [of God] might know the time of their visitation! There are many who have not yet heard the testing truth for this time. There are many with whom the Spirit of God is striving. The time of God's destructive judgments is the time of mercy for those who [until then] have [had] no opportunity to learn what is truth. Tenderly will the Lord look upon them. His heart of mercy is touched; His hand is still stretched out to save, while the door is closed to those who would not enter. Large numbers will be admitted who in these last days hear the truth for the first time.[145]—*TDG* 163.

God's Spirit will pass by those who have had their day of test and opportunity, but who have not distinguished the voice of God or appreciated the movings of His Spirit. Then thousands in the eleventh hour will see and acknowledge the truth.—*2SM* 16.

There was a shut door to the unbelievers in the destruction of Sodom, but an open door to Lot. There was a shut door to the inhabitants of Tyrus, a shut door to the inhabitants of Jerusalem . . . who disbelieved, but an open door to the humble, the believing, those who obeyed God. Thus it will be at the end of time. . . . These conversions will be made with a rapidity that will surprise the church, and God's name alone will be glorified.[146]—*TDG* 235.

Steps leading up to the close of human probation

There is an unerring record kept of the impieties of nations, of families, of individuals. God may bear long while the account goes on, and calls to repentance and offers of pardon may be given; yet a time will come when the account will be full, divine patience will be exercised no longer. Then the signal will be given for the wrath of offended justice to be poured out, for judgment to be executed.—*ST* 11 September 1884.

America Closes Her Probation

The people of the United States have been a favored people; but when they restrict religious liberty, surrender Protestantism, and give countenance to popery, the measure of their guilt will be full, and "national

---

145. *Testimonies for the Church,* 9:97, reads the same as this statement, except that it does not include this last sentence. (Cf *RH* 5 July 1906.)

146. These statements clearly show that *during* the time of God's destructive judgments, in other words, *during* "the seasons of calamity" (*3SM* 387) *before* probation closes, the door of mercy has closed for those who have had an opportunity to know present truth, such as Seventh-day Adventists, but who have either neglected it or rejected it, while it is still open for those who have never before known the third angel's message.

apostasy" will be registered in the books of heaven. The result of this apostasy will be national ruin.—*RH* 2 May 1893.

A time is coming when the law of God is, in a special sense, to be made void in . . . [America]. The rulers of . . . [the] nation will, by legislative enactments, enforce the Sunday law, and thus God's people [will] be brought into great peril. When our nation, in its legislative councils, shall enact laws to bind the consciences of men in regard to their religious privileges, enforcing Sunday observance, and bringing oppressive power to bear against those who keep the seventh-day Sabbath, the law of God will, to all intents and purposes, be made void in our land; and national apostasy will be followed by national ruin.—*RH* 18 December 1888.

Protestants will work upon the rulers of the land [America] to make laws to restore the lost ascendancy of the man of sin, who sits in the temple of God, showing himself that he is God. Roman Catholic principles will be taken under the care and protection of the state. This national apostasy will speedily be followed by national ruin. The protest of Bible truth will be no longer tolerated by those who have not made the law of God their rule of life. Then will the voice be heard from the graves of martyrs, represented by the souls that John saw slain for the word of God and the testimony of Jesus Christ which they held.—*RH* 15 June 1897.

By the decree enforcing the institution of the papacy in violation of the law of God, . . . [America] will disconnect herself fully from righteousness. When Protestantism shall stretch her hand across the gulf to grasp the hand of the Roman power, when she shall reach over the abyss to clasp hands with spiritualism, when, under the influence of this threefold union, our country shall repudiate every principle of its Constitution as a Protestant and republican government, and shall make provision for the propagation of papal falsehoods and delusions, then we may know that the time has come for the marvelous working of Satan and that the end is near.

As the approach of the Roman armies was a sign to the disciples of the impending destruction of Jerusalem, so may this apostasy be a sign to us that the limit of God's forbearance is reached, that the measure of our nation's iniquity is full, and that the angel of mercy is about to take her flight, never to return.—*5T* 451.

Foreign nations will follow the example of the United States. Though she leads out, yet the same crisis will come upon our people in all parts of the world.[147]—*6T* 395.

When human probation closes

It is in a crisis that character is revealed. . . . The great final test comes at the close of human probation, when it will be too late for the soul's need to be supplied.—*COL* 412.

When Jesus ceases to plead for man, the cases of all are forever decided . . . . Probation closes; Christ's intercessions cease in heaven. This time finally comes suddenly upon all, and those who have neglected to purify their souls by obeying the truth are found sleeping. . . .

If such had only known that the work of Christ in the heavenly sanctuary would close so soon, how differently would they have conducted themselves, how earnestly would they have watched! The Master, anticipating all this, gives them timely warning in the command to watch. He distinctly states the suddenness of His coming. He does not measure the time, lest we shall neglect a momentary preparation, and in our indolence look ahead to the time when we think He will come, and defer the preparation.—*2T* 191.

Men need to be aroused to realize the solemnity of the time, the nearness of the day when human probation shall be ended. God gives no man a message that it will be five years or ten years or twenty years before this earth's history shall close. He would not give any living being an excuse for delaying the preparation for his appearing. . . . Everyone who claims to be a servant of God is called to do his service as if each day might be the last.—*RH* 27 November 1900.

God has not revealed to us the time when this message will close, or when probation will have an end. Those things that are revealed we shall

---

147. What happens in America is a microcosm of what will happen in the world. For further discussion on this point, see the chapter "The Mark of the Beast and the Sunday Versus Sabbath Conflict."

accept for ourselves and for our children; but let us not seek to know that which has been kept secret in the councils of the Almighty. . . .

There is no command for anyone to search the Scriptures in order to ascertain, if possible, when probation will close. God has no such message for any mortal lips. He would have no mortal tongue declare that which He has hidden in His secret councils.—*RH* 9 October 1894.

In heaven the edict will soon go forth, "It is done." "He that is unjust, let him be unjust still: and he which is filthy, let him be filthy still: and he that is righteous, let him be righteous still: and he that is holy, let him be holy still. And, behold, I come quickly; and my reward is with me, to give every man according as his work shall be." Soon the last prayer for sinners will have been offered, the last tear shed, the last warning given, the last entreaty made, and the sweet voice of mercy will be heard no more.—*RH* 2 January 1900.

When the third angel's message closes, mercy no longer pleads for the guilty inhabitants of the earth. The people of God have accomplished their work. They have received "the latter rain," "the refreshing from the presence of the Lord," and they are prepared for the trying hour before them. . . . An angel returning from the earth announces that his work is done; the final test has been brought upon the world, and all who have proved themselves loyal to the divine precepts have received "the seal of the living God." Then Jesus ceases His intercession in the sanctuary above. He lifts His hands, and with a loud voice says, "It is done;" . . . "He that is unjust, let him be unjust still: and he which is filthy, let him be filthy still: and he that is righteous, let him be righteous still: and he that is holy, let him be holy still." Every case has been decided for life or death. . . .

When [Jesus] leaves the sanctuary, darkness covers the inhabitants of the earth.[148] In that fearful time the righteous must live in the sight of a holy God without an intercessor. The restraint which has been upon the wicked is removed, and Satan has entire control of the finally impenitent. God's

---

148. This is spiritual darkness, not literal darkness, for it falls *not* on the earth (see *GC* 635) but on "the inhabitants of the earth." (See also *GC* 491.) If this darkness were literal, God's people would know when probation closes, but this they do not know.

longsuffering has ended. . . . The wicked have passed the boundary of their probation; the Spirit of God, persistently resisted, has been at last withdrawn. Unsheltered by divine grace, they have no protection from the wicked one. Satan will then plunge the inhabitants of the earth into one great, final trouble. As the angels of God cease to hold in check the fierce winds of human passion, all the elements of strife will be let loose.—*GC* 613, 614.

The righteous and the wicked will still be living upon the earth in their mortal state—men will be planting and building, eating and drinking, all unconscious that the final, irrevocable decision has been pronounced in the sanctuary above. Before the flood, after Noah entered the ark, God shut him in, and shut the ungodly out; but for seven days the people, knowing not that their doom was fixed, continued their careless pleasure-loving life, and mocked the warnings of impending judgment. "So," says the Saviour, "shall also the coming of the Son of man be." Matthew 24:39. Silently, unnoticed as the midnight thief, will come the decisive hour which marks the fixing of every man's destiny, the final withdrawal of mercy's offer to guilty men.—*GC* 491.

The seven last plagues

When Christ shall cease His work as mediator in man's behalf, then this time of trouble will begin. Then the case of every soul will have been decided, and there will be no atoning blood to cleanse from sin. When Jesus leaves His position as man's intercessor before God, the solemn announcement is made, "He that is unjust, let him be unjust still: and he which is filthy, let him be filthy still; and he that is righteous, let him be righteous still; and he that is holy, let him be holy still." Revelation 22:11. Then the restraining spirit of God is withdrawn from the earth. As Jacob was threatened with death by his angry brother, so the people of God will be in peril from the wicked who are seeking to destroy them.—*PP* 201.

When our High Priest has finished His work in the sanctuary, He will stand up, put on the garments of vengeance, and then the seven last plagues will be poured out.—*EW* 36.

The bolts of God's wrath[149] are soon to fall, and when He shall begin to punish the transgressors, there will be no period of respite until the end.—*TM* 182.

In quick succession one angel after another will pour out vials of wrath upon the inhabitants of the earth.—*ST* 17 January 1900.

In the future there will be broken thrones and great distress of nations, with perplexity. Satan will work with intense activity. The earth will be filled with the shrieks of suffering, expiring nations. There will be war, war. The places of the earth will be in confusion, as from its bowels pours forth its burning contents, to destroy the inhabitants of the world.—*18MR* 92.

The people of God will then be plunged into those scenes of affliction and distress described by the prophet as the time of Jacob's trouble.—*GC* 616.

Satan . . . has set all his agents to work, that men may be deceived, deluded, occupied, and entranced, until the day of probation shall be ended, and the door of mercy be forever shut. The time is right upon us when there will be sorrow that no human balm can heal. Sentinel angels are now restraining the four winds, that they shall not blow till the servants of God are sealed in their foreheads; but when God shall bid his angels loose the winds, there will be a scene of strife such as no pen can picture.—*RH* 14 March 1912.

When Christ ceases His intercession in the sanctuary, the unmingled wrath threatened against those who worship the beast and his image and receive his mark [Revelation 14:9, 10], will be poured out. . . . Says the revelator, in describing those terrific scourges: "There fell a noisome and grievous sore upon the men which had the mark of the beast, and upon them which worshiped

---

149. These "bolts of God's wrath" are the seven last plagues, not the calamities that precede the close of probation, for there is no respite when these bolts of wrath begin to fall, whereas there will be a brief respite from the calamities around the time probation closes and before the plagues fall. (See *GC* 491.)

his image." The sea "became as the blood of a dead man; and every living soul died in the sea." And "the rivers and fountains of waters . . . became blood." Terrible as these inflictions are, God's justice stands fully vindicated. The angel of God declares: "Thou art righteous, O Lord, . . . because Thou hast judged thus. For they have shed the blood of saints and prophets, and Thou hast given them blood to drink; for they are worthy" [Revelation 16:2-6]. By condemning the people of God to death, they have as truly incurred the guilt of their blood as if it had been shed by their hands.[150]—*GC* 627, 628.

In the [fourth] plague that follows, power is given to the sun "to scorch men with fire. And men were scorched with great heat" [verses 7, 8]. The prophets thus describe the condition of the earth at this fearful time: "The land mourneth; . . . because the harvest of the field is perished." "All the trees of the field are withered: because joy is withered away from the sons of men." "The seed is rotten under their clods, the barns are laid desolate." "How do the beasts groan! the herds of cattle are perplexed, because they have no pasture. . . . The rivers of water are dried up, and the fire hath devoured the pastures of the wilderness." "The songs of the temple shall be howlings in that day, saith the Lord God: there shall be many dead bodies in every place: they shall cast them forth with silence" [Joel 1:10-12, 17-20; Amos 8:3].

These [first four] plagues are not universal,[151] or the inhabitants of the

---

150. Ellen White says: "these plagues enraged the wicked against the righteous; they thought that we had brought the judgments of God upon them, and that if they could rid the earth of us, the plagues would then be stayed. A decree went forth against the saints, which caused them to cry day and night for deliverance" (*EW* 36, 37). The second plague is probably falling *when* the edict goes forth to kill God's people. Because the third plague is poured out in retribution for this decree, and "these plagues" (more than one) have enraged the wicked against the righteous so that they issue a death decree, this seems to indicate that the decree is issued during the second plague, since there is no respite between the plagues.

151. The fact that the first four plagues are not universal seems to imply that the last three are. Thus, when the fifth plague falls, "a dense blackness, deeper than the darkness of the night falls upon the earth" (*GC* 636). The seventh plague is also clearly universal, for the mighty earthquake affects the entire planet.

The sixth plague is the drying up of "the great river Euphrates," not the Battle of Armageddon. The sixth plague falls when "the angry multitudes" (*GC* 636)—the waters upon which spiritual Babylon sits (Rev. 17:15)—realize they have been fighting against God and withdraw their support from spiritual Babylon. "When the voice of God turns the captivity of His people, there is a terrible awakening of those who have lost all in the great conflict of life" (*GC* 654). This withdrawal of support makes symbolic Babylon vulnerable to "capture" by the "kings of the east" (Rev. 16:12)—the Father and the Son at the Second Coming.

earth would be wholly cut off. Yet they will be the most awful scourges that have ever been known to mortals. All the judgments upon men, prior to the close of probation, have been mingled with mercy. . . , but in the final judgment, wrath is poured out unmixed with mercy. In that day, multitudes will desire the shelter of God's mercy which they have so long despised.—*GC* 628, 629.

Professed Christians during the time of Jacob's trouble

In these days of peril [the great time of trouble] those who have been unfaithful in their duties in life, and whose mistakes and sins of neglect are registered against them in the book in Heaven, unrepented of and unforgiven, will be overcome by Satan. . . . These will have no shelter in the time of Jacob's trouble. Their sins will then appear of such magnitude that they will have no confidence to pray, no heart to wrestle as did Jacob. On the other hand, those who have been of like passion, erring and sinful in their lives, but who have repented of their sins, and in genuine sorrow confessed them, will have pardon written against their names in the heavenly records. They will be hid in the day of the Lord's anger. Satan will attack this class, but like Jacob they have taken hold of the strength of God, and true to His character He is at peace with them, and sends angels to comfort and bless and sustain them in their time of peril. The time of Jacob's trouble will test every one, and distinguish the genuine Christian from the one who is so only in name.—*ST* 27 November 1879.

Those professed Christians who come up to that last fearful conflict [the time of Jacob's trouble] unprepared, will, in their despair, confess their sins in words of burning anguish, while the wicked exult over their distress.—*GC* 620.

Those who have been unfaithful in their duties in life, and whose mistakes and sins of neglect are registered against them in the book of Heaven, unrepented of and unforgiven, . . . will have no shelter in the time of Jacob's trouble. Their sins will then appear of such magnitude that they will have no confidence to pray.—*ST* 27 November 1879.

Those who have chosen the pleasures of the world and rebelled against God, will cry for mercy when there will be none to answer their prayers. . . .

[A]s they realize that they have no shelter from the dreadful storm of God's wrath, they will plead for one little hour of probation.—*YI* 1 January 1854.

God's true people during the great time of trouble

God . . . [will] in a wonderful manner preserve his people through the time of trouble. As Jesus poured out his soul in agony in the garden, they will earnestly cry and agonize with him day and night for deliverance. The decree will go forth that they must disregard the Sabbath of the fourth commandment and honor the first day, or lose their lives; but they will not yield, and trample under their feet the Sabbath of the Lord, and honor an institution of the Papacy.—*4bSG* 113.

In the time when God's judgments are falling without mercy, oh, how enviable to the wicked will be the position of those who abide "in the secret place of the Most High"—the pavilion in which the Lord hides all who have loved Him and have obeyed His commandments! The lot of the righteous is indeed an enviable one at such a time to those who are suffering because of their sins. But the door of mercy is closed to the wicked, no more prayers are offered in their behalf after probation ends.—*8MR* 193.

In the time of trouble none [of God's people] will labor with their hands. Their sufferings will be mental, and God will provide food for them.—*LDE* 265.

The people of God will not be free from suffering; but while persecuted and distressed, while they endure privation, and suffer for want of food, they will not be left to perish. . . . While the wicked are dying from hunger and pestilence, angels will shield the righteous and supply their wants. . . .

Yet to human sight it will appear that the people of God must soon seal their testimony with their blood, as did the martyrs before them. They themselves begin to fear that the Lord has left them to fall by the hands of their enemies. It is a time of fearful agony. Day and night they cry unto God for deliverance. . . .

Could men see with heavenly vision, they would behold companies of angels that excel in strength stationed about those who have kept the word of Christ's patience. With sympathizing tenderness, angels have witnessed their distress, and have heard their prayers.—*GC* 630.

Those who live in the last days must pass through an experience similar to that of Jacob [when he wrestled with the angel]. Foes will be all around them, ready to condemn and destroy. Alarm and despair will seize them, for it appears to them as to Jacob in his distress, that God himself has become an avenging enemy.—*ST* 27 November 1879.

The time of trouble is the crucible that is to bring out Christlike characters. It is designed to lead the people of God to renounce Satan and his temptations. The last conflict will reveal Satan to them in his true character, that of a cruel tyrant, and it will do for them what nothing else could do, up-root him entirely from their affections.—*RH* 12 August 1884.

Let none be discouraged in view of the severe trials to be met in the time of Jacob's trouble, which is yet before them. They are to work earnestly, anxiously, not for that time, but for today. What we want [lack] is . . . a personal experience now. In these precious closing hours of probation, we have a deep and living experience to gain. We shall thus form characters that will ensure our deliverance in the time of trouble.—*RH* 12 August 1884.

The universal death decree

I saw the leading men of the earth consulting together, and Satan and his angels busy around them. I saw a writing, copies of which were scattered in different parts of the land, giving orders that unless the saints should yield their peculiar faith, give up the Sabbath, and observe the first day of the week, the people were at liberty after a certain time to put them to death.—*EW* 282, 283.

Though a general [or universal[152]] decree has fixed the time when commandment-keepers may be put to death, their enemies will in some cases anticipate the decree, and before the time specified, will endeavor to take their lives.—*GC* 631.

---

152. *PK* 512. In other words, the death decree will be a worldwide edict.

The time of Jacob's trouble

[After probation closes] the people of God will . . . be plunged into those scenes of affliction and distress described by the prophet as the time of Jacob's trouble. "Thus saith the Lord: We have heard a voice of trembling, of fear, and not of peace. . . . All faces are turned into paleness. Alas! for that day is great, so that none is like it: it is even the time of Jacob's trouble; but he shall be saved out of it" [Jeremiah 30:5-7]. . . .

Satan . . . will stir up the wicked to destroy God's people in the time of trouble. . . . [H]e will urge his accusations against the people of God. He numbers the world as his subjects; but the little company who keep the commandments of God are resisting his supremacy. If he could blot them from the earth, his triumph would be complete. He sees that holy angels are guarding them, and he infers that their sins have been pardoned; but he does not know that their cases have been decided in the sanctuary above. He has an accurate knowledge of the sins which he has tempted them to commit, and he presents these before God in the most exaggerated light, representing this people to be just as deserving as himself of exclusion from the favor of God. . . . He claims them as his prey, and demands that they be given into his hands to destroy. . . .

Though God's people will be surrounded by enemies who are bent upon their destruction, yet the anguish which they suffer is not a dread of persecution for the truth's sake; they fear that every sin has not been repented of, and that through some fault in themselves they will fail to realize the fulfillment of the Saviour's promise, "I will keep thee from the hour of temptation, which shall come upon all the world" [Revelation 3:10]. If they could have the assurance of pardon, they would not shrink from torture or death; but should they prove unworthy, and lost their lives because of their own defects of character, then God's holy name would be reproached. . . .

They afflict their souls before God, pointing to their past repentance of their many sins, and pleading the Saviour's promise, "Let him take hold of My strength, that he may make peace with Me; and he shall make peace with Me" [Isaiah 27:5]. Their faith does not fail because their prayers are not immediately answered. Though suffering the keenest anxiety, terror, and distress, they do not cease their intercessions. They lay hold of the strength of God as Jacob laid hold of the Angel; And the language of their souls is, "I will not let Thee go, except Thou bless me." . . .

God will not cast off those who have been deceived, and tempted, and betrayed into sin, but who have returned unto Him with true repentance. While Satan seeks to destroy this class, God will send His angels to comfort and protect them in the time of peril. The assaults of Satan are fierce and determined, his delusions[153] are terrible; but the Lord's eye is upon His people, and His ear listens to their cries. Their affliction is great, the flames of the furnace seem about to consume them; but the Refiner will bring them forth as gold tried in the fire. God's love for His children during the period of their severest trial, is as strong and tender as in the days of their sunniest prosperity.—*GC* 616-621.

The "time of trouble such as never was," is soon to open upon us; and we shall need an experience which we do not now possess, and which many are too indolent to obtain. It is often the case that trouble is greater in anticipation than in reality; but this is not true of the crisis before us. The most vivid presentation cannot reach the magnitude of the ordeal. In that time of trial, every soul must stand for himself before God. [The faith of individual members of the church will be tested as though there were not another person in the world.][154]—*GC* 622.

Angelic protection during the time of trouble

As difficulties thicken about . . . [God's] people amid the perils of the last days, He sends His angels to walk all the way by our side, drawing us closer and still closer to the bleeding side of Jesus. And as the greater trials come, lesser trials are forgotten.—*OHC* 317.

In the day of fierce trial . . . [Jesus] will say, "Come, my people, enter thou into thy chambers, and shut thy doors about thee: hide thyself as it were for a little moment, until the indignation be overpast." What are the chambers in which they are to hide?—They are the protection of Christ and holy angels. The people of God are not at this time all in one place. They are

---

153. Satan's almost irresistible delusion *after* the close of probation will be his personation of the glorified Christ (see *GC* 624; cf *LDE* 165, quoted below).
154. *7BC* 983.

in different companies, and in all parts of the earth; and they will be tried singly, not in groups. Every one must stand the test for himself.—*RH* 19 November 1908.

One more effort, and then Satan's last device is employed. He hears the unceasing cry [of the saints] for Christ to come, for Christ to deliver them. This last strategy is to personate Christ, and make them think their prayers are answered.—*LDE* 165.

But the people of God will not be misled. The teachings of this false christ are not in accordance with the Scriptures. His blessing is pronounced upon the worshipers of the beast and his image, the very class upon whom the Bible declares that God's unmingled wrath shall be poured out.

And, furthermore, Satan is not permitted to counterfeit the manner of Christ's advent.[155] The Saviour has warned His people against deception upon this point, and has clearly foretold the manner of His second coming.—*GC* 625.

None of God's people lose their lives after probation closes

I saw that the people of God, who had faithfully warned the world of His coming wrath, would be delivered. God would not suffer the wicked to destroy[156] those who were expecting translation and who would not bow to the decree of the beast or receive his mark. I saw that if the wicked were permitted to slay the saints, Satan and all his evil host, and all who hate God, would be gratified. And oh, what a triumph it would be for his satanic majesty to have power, in the last closing struggle, over those who had so long waited to behold Him whom they loved.—*EW* 284.

The eye of God, looking down the ages, was fixed upon the crisis which His people are to meet, when earthly powers shall be arrayed against them. . . .

---

155. This doesn't mean that Satan won't try to imitate the Second Coming, but whatever he does will bear no comparison with the cataclysmic events associated with the true Second Coming.
156. The fact that the 144,000 are delivered from the death decree and that they are the ones "who faithfully warned the world" tends to support the conclusion that the 144,000 are the ones who "will be permitted to act a part in proclaiming . . . [the third angel's message] when it shall have swelled into a loud cry" (*HS* 155).

If the blood of Christ's faithful witnesses were shed at this time, it would not, like the blood of the martyrs, be as seed sown to yield a harvest for God. Their fidelity would not be a testimony to convince others of the truth; for the obdurate heart has beaten back the waves of mercy until they return no more. If the righteous were now left to fall a prey to their enemies, it would be a triumph for the prince of darkness. . . . Glorious will be the deliverance of those who have patiently waited for . . . [Christ's] coming, and whose names are written in the book of life.—*GC* 634.

CHAPTER **Ten**

DELIVERANCE, THE SPECIAL RESURRECTION, AND THE SECOND COMING

Events surrounding the Second Coming

There shall be a time of trouble, such as never was since there was a nation, even to that time. And at that time your people shall be delivered, every one who is found written in the book. And many of those who sleep in the dust of the earth shall awake, some to everlasting life, some to shame and everlasting contempt.—Dan. 12:1, 2, NKJV.

Christ was offered once to bear the sins of many. To those who eagerly wait for Him He will appear a second time, apart from sin, for salvation.—Heb. 9:28, NKJV.

Behold, He is coming with clouds, and every eye will see Him, and they also who pierced Him. And all the tribes of the earth will mourn because of Him.—Rev. 1:7, NKJV.

Then the sky receded as a scroll when it is rolled up, and every mountain and island was moved out of its place. And the kings of the earth, the great men, the rich men, the commanders, the mighty men, every slave and every free man, hid themselves in the caves and in the rocks of the mountains, and said to the mountains and rocks, "Fall on us and hide us from the face of Him who sits on the throne and from the wrath of the Lamb! For the great day of His wrath has come, and who is able to stand?"—Rev. 6:14-17, NKJV.

It will be said in that day: "Behold, this is our God; we have waited for Him, and He will save us. This is the Lord; we have waited for Him; we will be glad and rejoice in His salvation."—Isa. 25:9, NKJV.

The Lord himself will come down from heaven, with a loud command, with the voice of the archangel and with the trumpet call of God, and the dead in Christ will rise first. After that, we who are still alive and are left will be caught up with them in the clouds to meet the Lord in the air. And so we will be with the Lord forever.—1 Thess. 4:16, 17, NIV.

The wicked try to kill the saints, but angels protect them
In the time of trouble we all fled from the cities and villages, but were pursued by the wicked, who entered the houses of the saints with a sword. They raised the sword to kill us, but it broke and fell as powerless as a straw. Then we all cried day and night for deliverance, and the cry came up before God.—*EW* 34.

Houses and lands will be of no use to the saints in the [great] time of trouble, for they will then have to flee before infuriated mobs.—*EW* 56.

During the night a very impressive scene passed before me. There seemed to be great confusion and the conflict of armies. A messenger from the Lord stood before me, and said, "Call your household. I will lead you; follow me." He led me down a dark passage, through a forest, then through the clefts of mountains, and said, "Here you are safe." There were others who had been led to this retreat. The heavenly messenger said, "The time of trouble has come as a thief in the night, as the Lord warned you it would come."—*Mar* 270; *Ms* 153, 1905.

I saw the saints suffering great mental anguish. They seemed to be surrounded with the wicked inhabitants of earth. Every appearance was against them. Some began to fear that God had left them at last to perish by the hand of the wicked. But if their eyes could have been opened, they would have seen themselves surrounded by angels of God. Next came the multitude of the angry wicked, and next a mass of evil angels, hurrying on the wicked to slay the saints. But as they would attempt to approach them, they would first have to pass this company of mighty, holy angels, which was impossible. The angels of God were causing them to recede, and also causing the evil angels who were pressing around them, to fall back. It was an hour of terrible, fearful agony to the saints. They cried day and night unto God for deliverance. To outward appearance, there was no possibility of their escape. The wicked had already commenced their triumphing, and were crying out, Why don't [*sic*] your God deliver you out of our hands? Why don't you go up, and save your lives? The saints heeded them not. They were wrestling with God like Jacob.—*1SG* 202, 203.

The voice of God delivers His people

The people of God—some in prison cells, some hidden in solitary retreats in the forests and mountains—still plead for divine protection, while in every quarter companies of armed men, urged on by hosts of evil angels, are preparing for the work of death. It is now, in the hour of utmost extremity, that the God of Israel will interpose for the deliverance of His chosen.[157] . . .

With shouts of triumph, jeering, and imprecation, throngs of evil men are about to rush upon their prey, when lo, a dense blackness, deeper than the darkness of the night, falls upon the earth. Then a rainbow, shining with the glory from the throne of God, spans the heavens, and seems to encircle each praying company. The angry multitudes are suddenly arrested. Their mocking cries die away. The objects of their murderous rage are forgotten. . . .

---

157. Just before the voice of God delivers His people, the wicked are permitted to discover these hiding places, apparently to show the watching universe the lengths to which the wicked will go to destroy the saints.

It is at midnight[158] that God manifests His power for the deliverance of His people. The sun appears, shining in its strength. Signs and wonders follow in quick succession. The wicked look with terror and amazement upon the scene, while the righteous behold with solemn joy the tokens of their deliverance. Everything in nature seems turned out of its course. The streams cease to flow. Dark, heavy clouds come up, and clash against each other. In the midst of the angry heavens is one clear space of indescribable glory, whence comes the voice of God[159] like the sound of many waters, saying, "It is done."—*GC* 635, 636.

Dark, heavy clouds came up and clashed against each other. The atmosphere parted and rolled back; then we could look up through the open space in Orion, whence came the voice of God.—*EW* 41.

I saw a flaming cloud come where Jesus stood. Then Jesus . . . took His place on the cloud which carried Him to the East, where it first appeared to

---

158. As the fateful "midnight" hour strikes, we can imagine that God's people, some of them hidden in forests, others in mountain fastnesses, and still others in the dens and caves of the earth, will be intently watching for the "open space in Orion" (*EW* 41) to loom up on the eastern horizon. (See *EW* 15.) *Prophets and Kings,* 720, states that the saints "will catch the first light of . . . [Christ's] second appearing." There is a reason for this. They know where to look!

Because the voice of God is heard "at midnight" from "the open space in Orion" and the "eyes [of God's people are] drawn to the east" so that they "catch the first light of" the Second Coming, it is possible to calculate the season of the year when the voice of God delivers His people. Assuming that "the open space in Orion" is the Nebula of Orion, which many astronomers consider to be "the most beautiful [object] in the heavens" (Neal E. Howard, *The Telescope Handbook and Star Atlas* [New York: Thomas Y. Crowell, 1967], 194), according to the U.S. Naval Observatory, the day on which the Nebula of Orion breaks over the eastern horizon at midnight each year is September 22. This is the first day of fall in the northern hemisphere. If the open space includes the whole constellation of Orion, this would occur a few weeks later but still in the fall.

That the open space in Orion appears at midnight in the fall of the year may be significant. The Millerite preacher, Samuel S. Snow, correctly observed that the ancient Jewish festivals that related to the Second Coming, such as the Day of Atonement and the Feast of Tabernacles, occurred in the autumn (in the Northern Hemisphere). We should be cautious, however, about making too much of this astronomical fact lest it be concluded that it is possible to calculate the day and hour of Jesus' coming. This is impossible, for an indefinite "number of days" elapse from the time "the cloud [bearing Jesus passes] from the holiest to the east" (*DS* 14 Mar. 1846).

The foregoing conclusion assumes that the rotation of the earth remains constant as we know it now. This assumption appears to be justified in view of the fact that, *until* the seventh plague, when "the sun appears, shining in its strength" "at midnight" (*GC* 636), the Sunday vs. Sabbath controversy is still raging, suggesting that the diurnal cycle has not been disturbed.

159. This "space of indescribable glory, whence comes the voice of God," is the "open space in Orion" (*EW* 41).

the saints on earth—a small black cloud which was the sign of the Son of man.—*Mar* 287.

Soon our eyes were drawn to the east, for a small black cloud had appeared, about half as large as a man's hand, which we all knew was the sign of the Son of man.—*EW* 15.

[The] voice [of God] shakes the heavens and the earth. There is a mighty earthquake, "such as was not since men were upon the earth, so mighty an earthquake, and so great" [Rev. 16:17, 18]. The firmament appears to open and shut. The glory from the throne of God seems flashing through. The mountains shake like a reed in the wind, and ragged rocks are scattered on every side. There is a roar as of a coming tempest. The sea is lashed into fury. There is heard the shriek of the hurricane, like the voice of demons upon a mission of destruction. The whole earth heaves and swells like the waves of the sea. [The sea boils like a pot, and the whole earth is in terrible commotion.][160] Its surface is breaking up. Its very foundations seem to be giving way. Mountain chains are sinking. Inhabited islands disappear. The seaports that have become like Sodom for wickedness, are swallowed up by the angry waters. . . . Great hailstones, every one "about the weight of a talent," are doing their work of destruction. . . .

Graves are opened, and "many of them that sleep in the dust of the earth . . . awake, some to everlasting life, and some to shame and everlasting contempt" [Dan. 12:2]. All who have died in the faith of the third angel's message [keeping the Sabbath][161] come forth from the tomb glorified, to hear God's covenant of peace with those who have kept His law. "They also which pierced Him" [Rev. 1:7], those that mocked and derided Christ's dying agonies, and the most violent opposers of His truth and His people, are raised to behold Him in His glory, and to see the honor placed upon the loyal and obedient.—*GC* 637.

The captivity of the righteous is turned, and with sweet and solemn whisperings they say to one another: "We are delivered. It is the voice of

---

160. *1T* 354.
161. *EW* 285.

God."[162] With solemn awe they listen to the words of the voice. The wicked hear, but understand not the words of the voice of God. They fear and tremble, while the saints rejoice.—*1T* 354.

Other effects of the voice of God

The coming of the Son of Man . . . will not take place until after the mighty earthquake shakes the earth. After the people have heard the voice of God they are in despair and trouble such as never was since there was a nation, and in this the people of God will suffer affliction. The clouds of heaven will clash, and there will be darkness. Then that voice comes from heaven and the clouds begin to roll back like a scroll, and there is [seen] the bright, clear sign of the Son of Man. The children of God know what that cloud means.

The sound of music is heard, and as it nears [the earth], the graves are opened and the dead are raised and there are thousands of thousands and ten thousand times ten thousand of angels that compose that glory, and encircle the Son of Man. Those who have acted the most prominent part in the rejection and crucifixion of Christ come forth to see Him as He is, and those who have rejected Christ come up and see the saints glorified, and it is at that time that the saints are changed in a moment, in the twinkling of an eye, and are caught up to meet their Lord in the air.—*9MR* 251, 252.

Thick clouds still cover the sky; yet the sun now and then breaks through, appearing like the avenging eye of Jehovah. Fierce lightnings leap from the heavens, enveloping the earth in a sheet of flame. Above the terrific roar of thunder, voices, mysterious and awful, declare the doom of the wicked. The words spoken are not comprehended by all; but they are

---

162. When the voice of God is heard delivering His people, they are languishing in dungeons, hiding in dense forests, mountain fastnesses, or the dens and caves of the earth. At first, apparently, they only hear the voice of God, and their reaction is one of relief and joyous solemnity as they say, "We are delivered." They then emerge from their hiding places. As they do so they are overwhelmed at seeing in their mortal state the unveiled glory of Deity and are terror-stricken. This reaction, however, is only momentary, for the next instant they are glorified. This is the "marvelous change" that *The Great Controversy,* 639, says comes over them. They are then able to bear the outshining of Deity in all its splendor.

distinctly understood by the false teachers. Those who a little before were so reckless, so boastful and defiant, so exultant in their cruelty to God's commandment-keeping people, are now overwhelmed with consternation, and shuddering in fear. Their wails are heard above the sound of the elements. Demons acknowledge the deity of Christ, and tremble before His power, while men are supplicating for mercy, and groveling in abject terror. . . .

Through a rift in the clouds, there beams a star whose brilliancy is increased fourfold in contrast with the darkness.—*GC* 637, 638.

In the day of . . . [Christ's] coming, the last great trumpet is heard, and there is a terrible shaking of earth and heaven. The whole earth, from the loftiest mountains to the deepest mines, will hear. Everything will be penetrated by fire. The tainted atmosphere will be cleansed by fire. The fire having fulfilled its mission, the dead that have been laid away in the grave will come forth—some to the resurrection of life, to be caught up to meet their Lord in the air, and some to behold the coming of Him whom they have despised, and whom they now recognize as the Judge of all the earth.

All the righteous are untouched by the flames. . . . Earthquakes, hurricanes, flames, and flood cannot injure those who are prepared to meet their Saviour in peace.—*UL* 261.

When the earth shall reel to and fro like a drunkard, when it shall be removed as a cottage, when the great men and the proud men and those who have made the world their god shall cast their idols of gold and silver to the moles and to the bats, and shall go into the caves and dens of the earth, there will be those who will cry for the rocks and mountains to fall on them, and hide them "from the face of Him that sitteth upon the throne, and from the wrath of the Lamb" (Revelation 6:16).—*Ms* 12, 1895.

Before the glory of Him who is to reign the mountains will tremble and bow, the rocks will be removed out of their place, for once more will the Lord shake, not alone the earth, but the heavens also. The scattered ones who have fled for their lives to the rocks, the dens, the caverns of the earth, because of the violence of their adversaries will be made glad at the voice of God. . . .

The child of God will be terror-stricken at the first sight of the majesty of Jesus Christ. He feels that he cannot live in His holy presence. But the Word comes to him as to John, "Fear not." Jesus laid His right hand upon John; He raised him up from his prostrate position. So will He do unto His loyal trusting ones, for there are greater revelations of the glory of God to be given them.—*TMK* 360; cf *EW* 16.

The hidden ones have been scattered because of man's enmity against the law of Jehovah. They have been oppressed by all the powers of the earth. They have been scattered in the dens and caves of the earth through the violence of their adversaries, because they are true and obedient to Jehovah's laws. But deliverance comes to the people of God. To their enemies God will show Himself a God of just retribution. . . .

From the dens and caves of the earth, that have been the secret hiding places of God's people, they are called forth as His witnesses, true and faithful.

The people who have braved out their rebellion will fulfill the description given in Revelation 6:15-17. In these very caves and dens [where God's people have been hiding] they will find the very statement of truth in the letters and in the publications[163] as witness against them. The shepherds who lead the sheep in false paths will hear the charge made against them: "It was you who made light of truth. It was you who told us that God's law was abrogated, that it was a yoke of bondage. It was you who voiced the false doctrines when I was convicted that these Seventh-

---

163. It is evident that God's people take the writings of the Spirit of Prophecy with them into their hiding places. After the mighty earthquake ceases, the wicked read these "letters and . . . publications," which the saints have left behind, because they have no further need of them. We can imagine that the saints have preserved these writings at the risk of their lives (Rev. 20:4), and they have doubtless marked them and left them open to the places where they last used them. What a revelation these letters and publications will be to the lost!

Observe that God's people are still called "Seventh-day Adventists"! This is encouraging. But it should lead no Seventh-day Adventist to take presumptuous pride in this fact. And yet, it answers the question: Does Seventh-day Adventism survive the perils of the coming crisis until the Second Coming? It does, but not necessarily with the same organizational structure as it has today. The organization of the church invisible remains intact, but it is highly unlikely that the organization of the church visible survives in the form we know it.

day Adventists had the truth. The blood of our souls is upon your priestly garments."[164]—*Mar* 290.

The day and hour of Jesus' coming announced

The voice of God is heard from heaven, declaring the day and hour of Jesus' coming, and delivering the everlasting covenant to His people. Like peals of loudest thunder, His words roll through the earth.—*GC* 640.

The living saints, 144,000 in number, knew and understood the voice, while the wicked thought it was thunder and an earthquake.[165]—*EW* 15.

[God] spoke one sentence, and then paused, while the words were rolling through the earth. The Israel of God stood with their eyes fixed upward, listening to the words as they came from the mouth of Jehovah and rolled through the earth . . . It was awfully solemn. At the end of every sentence the saints shouted, "Glory! Hallelujah!"—*EW* 285, 286.

A glorious light shone upon . . . [the saints]. How beautiful they then looked. All marks of care and weariness were gone, and health and beauty were seen in every countenance. Their enemies, the heathen around them, fell like dead men; they could not endure the light that shone upon the delivered, holy ones.—*EW* 272, 273.

The clouds sweep back, and the starry heavens are seen, unspeakably glorious in contrast with the black and angry firmament on either side. The glory of the celestial city streams from the gates ajar. Then there

---

164. *Suggested sequence of events:* Apparently these final, critical, cataclysmic events occur in the following order: (1) God permits the wicked to find the places where His people have been hiding, shortly *before* the death decree is to go into effect; (2) As midnight strikes and the wicked rush in for the kill, they are arrested by "a dense blackness, deeper than the darkness of the night" (*GC* 636); (3) At the last moment, midnight, God turns tables on the persecutors of His people and delivers His beleaguered saints by uttering His voice from "the open space in Orion" (*EW* 41); (4) There is a mighty earthquake; (5) Terror-stricken, the wicked flee into the very caves where God's people have been hiding, probably because it is the closest shelter at hand; (6) We may well imagine that as they flee, they pass God's people emerging from these caves, joyful at being delivered and eagerly anticipating meeting their Lord; (6) While these events are transpiring, the special resurrection takes place.
165. These "words . . . are distinctly understood by the false teachers" (*GC* 638).

appears against the sky a hand holding two tables of stone folded together. . . . The hand opens the tables, and there are seen the precepts of the decalogue, traced as with a pen of fire. The words are so plain that all can read them. Memory is aroused, the darkness of superstition and heresy is swept from every mind, and God's ten words, brief, comprehensive, and authoritative, are presented to the view of all the inhabitants of the earth.—*GC* 639.

When God's temple in heaven is opened, what a triumphant time that will be for all who have been faithful and true![166] In the temple will be seen the ark of the testament in which were placed the two tables of stone, on which are written God's law. These tables of stone will be brought forth from their hiding place, and on them will be seen the Ten Commandments engraved by the finger of God. These tables of stone now lying in the ark of the testament will be a convincing testimony to the truth and binding claims of God's law.—*7BC* 972.

The sign of the Son of Man

We heard the voice of God which shook the heavens and earth, and gave the 144,000 the day and hour of Jesus' coming. Then the saints were free, . . . for . . . [God] had turned their captivity. And I saw a flaming cloud come where Jesus stood and he laid off His priestly garment and put on his kingly robe, took his place on the cloud, which carried him to the east, where it first appeared to the saints on earth, a small black cloud, which was the sign of the Son of man. While the cloud was passing from the Holiest to the east, which took a number of days, the synagogue of Satan worshiped at the saints' feet.—*DS* 14 March 1846.

Our eyes were drawn to the east, for a small black cloud had appeared, about half as large as a man's hand, which we all knew was the sign of the Son of man. We all in solemn silence gazed on the cloud as it drew nearer

---

166. God's people triumph when the voice of God turns the captivity of His people. It is *after* this that "God's temple in heaven is opened . . . [and] in the temple . . . [is] seen the ark of the testament" with "the two tables of stone," on which are "engraved" the "Ten Commandments."

and became lighter, glorious, and still more glorious, till it was a great white cloud. The bottom appeared like fire; a rainbow was over the cloud, while around it were ten thousand angels, singing a most lovely song; and upon it sat the Son of man.—*EW* 15, 16.

At first we did not see Jesus on the cloud, but as it drew near the earth we could behold His lovely person.—*EW* 35.

All heaven will be emptied of the angels, while the saints will be looking for . . . [Christ] and gazing into heaven, as were the men of Galilee when He ascended from the Mount of Olivet. Then only those who are holy, those who have followed fully the meek Pattern, will with rapturous joy exclaim as they behold Him, "Lo, this is our God; we have waited for Him, and He will save us."[167] And they will be changed "in a moment, in the twinkling of an eye, at the last trump."—*EW* 110.

No human language can portray the scenes of the second coming of the Son of Man in the clouds of heaven. He is to come with his own glory, and with the glory of the Father and of the holy angels. He will come clad in the robe of light, which he has worn from the days of eternity.—*RH* 5 September 1899.

Ten thousand times ten thousand and thousands of thousands of angels, the beautiful, triumphant sons of God, possessing surpassing loveliness and glory, will escort him on his way. . . . In the place of that old purple robe, he will be clothed in a garment of whitest white, "so as no fuller on earth can white" it [Mark 9:3]. And on his vesture and on his thigh a name will be written, "King of kings, and Lord of lords" [Rev. 19:16].—*RH* 13 November 1913.

---

167. The wicked have been deceived by satanic personations of various kinds, but not God's people. When Satan personates Christ (*GC* 624), the wicked exclaim, "Christ has come! Christ has come!" (*GC* 624). (See John 5:43, NASB.) But God's people are not misled. They patiently (Rev. 14:12) wait for their Lord to appear, and now, as they recognize Him coming in the clouds of heaven, they exclaim, "Lo, *this* is our God. We have waited for *him* and he will save us" (Isa. 25:9, emphasis supplied).

When the Second Advent judgment sits

Christ would have all understand the events of His second coming. The judgment[168] scene will take place in the presence of all the worlds; for in this judgment the government of God will be vindicated, and His law will stand forth as "holy, just, and good." Then every case will be decided, and sentence will be passed upon all.—*RH* 20 September 1898.

The hour of Judgment[169] is almost here,—long delayed by the goodness and mercy of God. But the trump of God will sound to the consternation of the unprepared who are living, and awaken the pale nations of the dead. The great white throne will appear, and all the righteous dead will come forth to immortality.—*RH* 24 May 1887.

The Son of man will come in the clouds of heaven with his own glory, with the glory of His Father,[170] and the glory of the holy angels. The law of God will be revealed in its majesty; and those who have stood in defiant rebellion against its holy precepts will understand that the law that they have discarded, and despised, and trampled underfoot is God's standard of character.[171] . . . Those who have ministered in word and doctrine; who by smooth words and fair speeches have taught that the law of God is no longer binding, that the Sabbath of the fourth

---

168. The Bible plainly teaches that there will be a judgment at Christ's second coming (2 Tim 4:5). It is at this judgment that "every case will be decided, and sentence passed upon all." The sentence, however, is not executed until *after* the millennium.

169. The fact that this speaks of "the unprepared who are living" and of "all the righteous dead . . . [who] come forth to immortality" establishes that this is the Second-Advent judgment.

170. Christ told Caiaphas that he would "see the Son of Man sitting at the right hand of the Mighty One and coming on the clouds of heaven" (Matt. 26:64, NIV). The only person the Mighty One could possibly be is God the Father.

171. At the Second Coming Christ comes in the clouds of heaven with His own glory, with the glory of His Father, and with the glory of all the holy angels. "The law of God," which is "revealed in its majesty" at this time, is the law that contains "the Sabbath of the fourth commandment." In other words, it is the Ten-Commandment law.

The fact that "those who have ministered in word and doctrine; who by smooth words and fair speeches have taught that the law of God is no longer binding . . . will have brought to their minds the scenes of Sinai in all their grandeur" shows that these people are the living lost. It follows, therefore, these are people who have been alive *throughout* the Sunday vs. Sabbath conflict, which begins *before* the close of probation and *culminates* when the tables of the Ten Commandments appear in the sky. (Cf *ST* 14 November 1895, quoted under the subhead *The Tables of Stone of the Original Law Will Be the Standard.*)

commandment was given for the Jews only; who have educated their hearers to show contempt for the warnings sent by the Lord's prophets and apostles and delegated servants, will have brought to their minds the scenes of Sinai in all their grandeur.—*RH* 22 November 1898.

When the judgment shall sit, and the books shall be opened, and every man shall be judged according to the things written in the books, then the tables of stone, hidden by God until that day,[172] will be presented before the world as the standard of righteousness.—*RH* 28 January 1909.

There is a sanctuary, and in that sanctuary is the ark, and in the ark are the tables of stone, on which are written the law spoken from Sinai amidst scenes of awful grandeur. These tables of stone are in the heavens,[173] and they will be brought forth in that day when the judgment shall sit and the books shall be opened, and men shall be judged according to the things written in the books. They will be judged by the law written by the finger of God and given to Moses to be deposited in the ark.—*20MR* 68.

---

172. "The tables of stone hidden by God until" "the judgment shall sit," when they "are presented to the world as the standard of righteousness," are the original tables of the law, not the copy given to Moses, for Moses and others saw the tables of the law God gave him, but no mortal, except the prophets of God in vision, have seen the original tables of the law (e.g., *1T* 76). These tables for the first time are seen by the inhabitants of earth at Christ's second coming, when, according to *The Great Controversy,* 639, they appear in the sky. *"Until"* that day—the day "God's temple in heaven is opened" and "these tables of stone . . . [are] brought forth from their hiding place" (*7BC* 972)—they remain "hidden." This conclusion is confirmed by the statement in *Manuscript Releases,* 20:68, which follows.

173. *The Great Controversy* states that "The law of God in the sanctuary in heaven is the great original, of which the precepts inscribed on tables of stone, and recorded by Moses in the Pentateuch, were an unerring transcript." These tables of stone, which were given to Moses, were placed in the ark of the testament (*1BC* 1109). Ellen White states that in Jeremiah's time (ca 592 B.C.) some of "the righteous in Jerusalem" "secreted" this "sacred ark containing the tables of stone on which had been traced the precepts of the Decalogue" "in a cave," and she adds, that this ark "has never been disturbed since it was secreted" (*PK* 453). "But in God's appointed time He will bring forth these tables of stone to be a testimony to all the world against the disregard of His commandments and against the idolatrous worship of the counterfeit Sabbath" (*1MR* 1109).

One thing is clear beyond question: The "tables of stone [which] are in the [sanctuary in the] heavens" are *not* the tables of stone secreted in a cave here on earth. "The law" mentioned in *Manuscript* 20, 1906, quoted above is *the writing on the tables of stone in the ark in the heavenly sanctuary, not the tables of stone themselves.* Proof that this is correct appears in *The Signs of the Times,* 28 February 1878 and the *Review and Herald,* 14 November 1895, both quoted below.

The original tables of stone containing God's law is the standard

Sacrilegious minds and hearts have thought they were mighty enough to change the times and laws of Jehovah; but safe in the archives of heaven, in the ark of God, are the original commandments, written upon the two tables of stone. No potentate of earth has power to draw forth those tables from their sacred hiding place beneath the mercy-seat.[174]—*ST* 28 February 1878.

The original law of God is safely deposited in the ark in the heavenly sanctuary, and will be presented to man just as God engraved it on the tables of stone. . . . The fourth commandment will be found in the bosom of the Decalogue just as it was written by the finger of God, and every soul who has presumed to exalt the false sabbath above the Sabbath which was sanctified and blessed and given to mankind for respect and observance, will be found out of harmony with the law of God. . . . Those who have knowingly trampled upon the true Sabbath, while they have exalted to its place a spurious institution, will have to answer for their action before the Lord who made heaven and earth, the sea, and all that is therein.[175]—*ST* 14 November 1895.

It is impossible to describe the horror and despair of those who have trampled upon God's holy requirements.[176] . . .

---

174. During the Sunday vs. Sabbath controversy *before* the close of probation, "sacrilegious minds and hearts have thought that they were mighty enough to change the times and laws of Jehovah." In fact, "the powers of earth" have endeavored to substitute "the laws of men for the law of God" (*RH* 23 April 1901), but they have not been able to touch the "original commandments," which are "safe in the archives of heaven."

175. These are obviously people who are alive at the Second Coming. If they are alive then, they were alive when "the false sabbath" was exalted before the close of probation. Yet they "knowingly trampled upon the true Sabbath" and they "will have to answer for their action before the Lord," when "the original law of God . . . in the heavenly sanctuary . . . [is] presented to man." (Cf *RH* 22 November 1898, quoted above.)

176. One can imagine the consternation of the lost when "the original commandments" appear in the sky. *During* the Sunday vs. Sabbath controversy, when God brings forth, or permits men to bring forth, the "copy" of His "law" (*1BC* 1109) from "a cave" here on earth (*PK* 453)—the tables of stone, which "He gave to Moses," "to be a testimony to all the world against the disregard of His commandments and against the idolatrous worship of the counterfeit Sabbath" (*1BC* 1109)—"those who . . . stood in defiant rebellion against his holy precepts will understand that the law that they have discarded, and despised, and trampled underfoot is God's holy standard of character" (*RH* 22 November 1898). "Too late they see that the Sabbath of the fourth commandment is the seal of the living God"! (*GC* 639).

The enemies of God's law, from the ministers down to the least among them, have a new conception of truth and duty. Too late they see that the Sabbath of the fourth commandment is the seal of the living God.—*GC* 639, 640.

The general resurrection of the righteous dead

The King of kings descends upon the cloud, wrapped in flaming fire. The heavens are rolled together as a scroll, the earth trembles before Him, and every mountain and island is moved out of its place. . . .

Amid the reeling of the earth, the flash of lightning, and the roar of thunder, the voice of the Son of God calls forth the sleeping saints. He looks upon the graves of the righteous, then raising His hands to heaven He cries, "Awake, awake, awake, ye that sleep in the dust, and arise!" Throughout the length and breadth of the earth, the dead shall hear that voice; and they that hear shall live. And the whole earth shall ring with the tread of the exceeding great army of every nation, kindred, tongue, and people. From the prison-house of death they come, clothed with immortal glory, crying, "O death, where is thy sting? O grave, where is thy victory?" [1 Corinthians 15:55]. And the living righteous and the risen saints unite their voices in a long, glad shout of victory.

All come forth from their graves the same in stature as when they entered the tomb. . . . But all arise with the freshness and vigor of eternal youth. . . . The mortal, corruptible form, devoid of comeliness, once polluted with sin, becomes perfect, beautiful, and immortal. All blemishes and deformities are left in the grave.—*GC* 641-645.

Mortality puts on immortality and corruption puts on incorruption

The living righteous are changed "in a moment, in the twinkling of an eye." At the voice of God they were glorified; now they are made immortal, and with the risen saints are caught up to meet their Lord in the air. Angels "gather together the elect from the four winds, from one end of heaven to the other."—*GC* 645.

The 144,000 shouted, "Alleluia!" as they recognized their friends who had been torn from them by death.—*EW* 16.

As the little infants come forth immortal from their dusty beds, they immediately wing their way to their mother's arms.—*2SM* 260.

Friends long separated by death are united, nevermore to part, and with songs of gladness ascend together to the city of God.—*GC* 645.

Ascension to the sea of glass

We all entered the cloud together, and were seven days ascending to the sea of glass.[177]—*EW* 16.

---

177. Because the journey to the sea of glass takes seven days, all the redeemed will have kept at least one Sabbath before they enter heaven.

May it be our blessed privilege to "escape all these things [predicted to] come to pass [before the Second Coming] and to stand before the Son of man" (Luke 21:36), clothed in His righteousness.